The American Illustrated Cook Book of

SOUPS

by Anne Tynte

CONTENTS

Published by Doubleday & Company, Inc.
Under arrangement with Ottenheimer Publishers, Inc.

ISBN: 0-385-02330-8

INTRODUCTION

Making Soup

In this book you will find a great variety of soups, from clear consommes, creamy vegetable soups and delicately flavored iced soups to thick meat and vegetable soups and chowders, which are sufficiently filling and nutritious to be served as a meal in themselves. You will also find rich party soups and continental fruit soups, not to mention the numerous nourishing everyday soups.

They are all interesting to make as well as tasty and nearly all are simple to prepare if you are an imaginative cook, you can turn them into at least twice this number by your own original additions and variations.

If you are not already a convinced soup-maker I hope this book will inspire you to become one, because what can be more warming on a cold winter's night than a bowl of richly-flavored and aromatic steaming home-made soup? Soup also has its place in summer when appetites are jaded. A light iced concoction can revive the spirits and make the perfect beginning for a summer party menu.

The advent of stock cubes has made soup-making a great deal simpler for the hurried cook but it is well worth making your own stock, too, and keeping a supply, ready for use at any time. Home-made stock is simple to make, is the perfect base for so many soups, and can easily be stored in a deep freeze.

If you are a soup-maker already you will know that it is never necessary to throw away even small scraps left over from the serving dish after a meal. These can all be carefully saved and used as garnishes for soups or, in innumerable combinations, can form the basis of many interesting soups. Do not be afraid to experiment, all sorts of unlikely foods combined in an electric blender and mixed with stock and water make excellent soups.

Cream soups can be made in two ways. In each case the vegetable concerned is cooked slowly by itself or in combinations with other vegetables until it is tender. It is then converted to a purée by being put through a food mill or nylon sieve or, better still, an electric blender. In one method this purée is mixed with a thin white sauce mixture and heated together without boiling until hot enough to serve. A liaison of egg yolks and cream can be added to enrich and slightly thicken the soup if desired. If this done the soup must on no account be boiled or the egg will curdle or scramble and the creamy texture will be ruined. In the second method (which is the one most used in this book) the thickening flour is added to the vegetables and the liquid. The whole lot are then cooked together before being puréed.

Spring Soup *(see p. 8)*

Storing Soup in a Deep Freeze

Soup can be made and stored successfully in a deep freeze as long as the following points are noted:

1. Where a recipe gives all purpose flour as an ingredient substitute cornstarch and reduce the quantity from 1 tablespoon to 1½—2 teaspoons. Cornstarch freezes much more satisfactorily than plain flour.

2. In order to take up as little valuable freezing space as possible in the freezer it is more sensible to make the soups with the minimum of liquid, just sufficient to make a thick purée. The remaining liquid indicated in the recipe can then be added at the time of re-heating. This usually also gives the soup a fresher flavor, another bonus point.

3. Do not freeze for longer than necessary soups which contain a high proportion of onions, garlic or herbs, as these develop a rather strong and unpleasant flavor if kept for more than four weeks.

4. To keep carefully prepared stock for later use, reduce the quantity by simmering gently with the lid off the pan until a very concentrated broth remains. This can be frozen in ice cube sections or small bags or freezer containers. The cubes are then used in soups or other dishes after the addition of water to return to correct strength.

5. Jellied soups do not keep well in a freezer as gelatine is affected adversely by the action of freezing.

6. It is inadvisable to freeze soups containing chunks of cucumber, squash or zucchini as these do not freeze successfully.

7. Garnishes for soups, such as croutons, chopped herbs, shredded orange and lemon rind, grated cheese and chopped cooked ham, can all be stored in the freezer, which saves a great deal of time when you have to prepare a meal unexpectedly.

Shrimp Bisque (see p. 32)

2 STOCKS

Chicken Stock for Consomme

- 1 boiling chicken with giblets
- 2 peeled and sliced onions
- 4 stalks of celery
- 2–3 carrots
- 1 thin sliver of lemon rind
- 1 bay leaf
- 6–8 sprigs of parsley
- 1 sprig of tarragon (or ¼ teaspoon dried tarragon)
- 1 small sprig of thyme (or ¼ teaspoon dried thyme)
- 6 peppercorns
- 1 teaspoon salt (or more if needed)

1. Put a cleaned and cut-up boiling chicken into a large pot with sliced vegetables. Add the herbs and seasoning. Cover with water, and bring slowly to a boil. Then cover pan and simmer for 2 hours until all the flavor is in the soup.

2. Strain and let cool. When cold, skim fat from the top and use the stock for chicken consomme or other soups requiring strong chicken stock. The stock can also be stored in the deep freeze.

Ordinary Chicken Stock

1 cooked chicken carcass
giblets, if available
1 onion, sliced
2 carrots, sliced
2 stalks of celery
1 bay leaf
1 sprig of thyme (or ¼ teaspoon dried thyme)
6 sprigs of parsley
6 peppercorns
1 chicken cube (if necessary)

1. Put the broken-up chicken carcass and bones into a pan with any available giblets and any left-over chicken meat or skin. Add the vegetables and herbs. Cover with water, and add pepper and salt. Bring to a boil slowly, and simmer for 1–2 hours, or until well flavored. If not sufficiently well flavored add a chicken cube and cook for a few more minutes.

2. Strain and let cool. If not using at once store in the refrigerator, boiling it up daily, or in a deep freeze.

Game Stock

1 game carcass with any meat attached
2 onions sliced
2 carrots sliced
2–3 stalks of celery
6 sprigs of parsley
1 sprig of thyme (or ¼ teaspoon dried thyme)
1 bay leaf
6–8 peppercorns

1. Put the carcass of the game bird into a pan with the sliced vegetables, herbs and seasoning. Cover with water and bring slowly to a boil. Then skim off any scum that rises to the surface, and simmer until well flavored and reduced in quantity.

2. Strain and use or freeze for later use.

White Bone Stock

2 pounds raw veal knuckle bones
1 chicken carcass and giblets
2 onions, peeled and sliced
2 carrots, peeled and sliced
3 stalks of celery
1 bay leaf
1 bay leaf
6 sprigs of parsley
1 small sprig of thyme (or ¼ teaspoon dried thyme)
2 teaspoons salt
6 peppercorns
1 small piece of mace
3 quarts water
rind of ½ lemon

1. Have butcher chop the raw veal bones and chicken carcass into small pieces. Put these into pan of water with vegetables, herbs and seasoning. Bring to a boil and skim frequently for about half an hour. Add 1 cup cold water and skim again. Then add lemon rind and simmer for 2 hours.

2. Strain through muslin and sieve. Then let cool. Remove the fat from the top. Use at once, keep in covered bowl in refrigerator or freeze.

Creole Soup (see p. 10)

Fish Stock

½–1 pound fish back-bones and skins
1 onion sliced
2 small carrots sliced
2 stalks celery
6 sprigs of parsley
1 bay leaf
1 sprig of thyme
6–7 cups water
1½ cups white wine or cider (optional)

1. Use back-bones from white fish—sole, turbot or halibut preferably—and the skins if available. Put these in a pan with the sliced onion, carrot, celery, herbs and water. Add the white wine or cider if available. Then add salt and pepper. Bring very slowly to a boil and simmer for 30–40 minutes until the liquid has reduced and is well flavored.

2. Strain and cool. Use at once or freeze for later use.

Rich Brown Beef Stock

- 2–3 pounds veal bones
- 2–3 pounds meaty beef bones (including a bone with marrow)
- 2 pounds of lean beef—in one piece for boiled beef or cut into pieces
- 3–4 onions unpeeled or 2 onions and 2 leeks
- 4 carrots
- 4 stalks of celery
- 10 peppercorns
- a few mushroom stalks or peelings
- 2 bay leaves
- 8–10 sprigs of parsley
- 1 sprig of thyme (or ¼ teaspoon dried thyme)
- 5 quarts water

1. Get butcher to break bones. Put them into a pan with the beef and a little beef marrow or good dripping. Heat the pan, and as the bones and meat brown, stir and keep from burning. Remove and keep warm while browning the vegetables. Return the bones and meat to pan, and cover with water. Add herbs, salt, pepper, and mushroom peelings or stems if available.

2. Bring to a boil. Skim frequently during the first hour. Then cover pan and simmer for 2–3 hours, by which time the stock should be well flavored and a good brown color. (If the meat is a large piece and is to be used as boiled beef this can be removed after 2 hours, and the stock simmered without it for remaining cooking time.)

3. Strain the stock and let cool. Then skim off the fat, which will form a crust on top. If the stock is not required for a day or two, do not remove fat until just before using, as it acts as a protective seal. Keep in a refrigerator or deep freeze.

Vegetable Stock

- 3 medium onions, unpeeled
- 3 medium carrots, peeled
- 2 leeks, white part only
- 4–5 stalks of celery
- 1 small turnip, peeled
- 1 tablespoon butter or oil
- 2–3 quarts water
- 6 peppercorns
- 1 bay leaf
- 4–6 sprigs of parsley
- 1 sprig of thyme (or ¼ teaspoon dried thyme)

1. Cut up the vegetables and brown these until golden in either a little butter or oil. Add water, herbs and seasoning. Bring to a boil, and simmer for 1½–2 hours, by which time the stock should be well flavored.

2. Strain and cool. Use for soups or sauces calling for vegetable stock.

Mixed Household Stock

- 2 pounds mixed raw or cooked beef, veal and/or chicken bones and possibly a ham bone
- 1½ pounds of onions, carrots, celery, chopped
- a little oil
- 1 bay leaf
- 6 sprigs of parsley
- 1 sprig of thyme
- a few mushroom stalks or peelings
- 6–8 peppercorns

Stock made from mixed raw and cooked bones, either beef, veal, chicken, or ham but not mutton or pork, as these have a rather strong flavor

1. Brown the raw bones and the vegetables in a little hot oil. Then add the cooked bones, herbs, mushroom peelings. Add water to cover and bring to a boil. Then simmer for 1½–2 hours until reduced and well flavored.

2. Strain and cool, allowing the fat to set in a solid crust on top. Use this stock quickly or keep in a freezer. If keeping in a refrigerator for a day or two re-boil every day to keep it from becoming sour.

3 VEGETABLE SOUPS

Spring Soup

A delicious soup full of fresh spring vegetables, enriched with egg yolk and cream (Serves 4–6, hot–see picture, p. 3)

4 young carrots
2–3 young leeks according to size (or 8–10 scallions)
3 tablespoons butter
1½ tablespoons flour
4 cups chicken stock (or water and chicken cubes)
½ cup cauliflower flowerets
2–3 tablespoons peas
2–3 tablespoons young green beans
a little sugar
2 tablespoons mixed parsley, chervil, mint and thyme

LIAISON
½ cup cream
2 egg yolks

1. Peel and dice the carrots. Wash the leeks or scallions thoroughly and cut the white part into slices. Melt the butter and cook these vegetables gently in a covered pan for 5–6 minutes without allowing to brown. Sprinkle in flour, mix thoroughly, then add stock. Blend well until smooth and bring to a boil, stirring constantly. Cook for a few minutes before adding cauliflower flowerets, peas, sliced beans and sugar. Simmer for 15 minutes. Add the herbs, and cook for a few more minutes, to draw out flavor of the herbs. Season to taste.

2. Make the liaison by mixing the cream with the egg yolks. Take a few spoonsful of the hot soup and mix well with the cream and egg yolk mixture before straining it back into the soup, stirring constantly. Reheat, being very careful not to allow soup to boil as this causes egg to curdle and spoils the texture of the soup.

Minestrone

A richly varied vegetable soup originally from Italy, garnished with grated Italian cheese (Serves 6–8, hot)

½ cup dried haricot or soup beans
2–3 tablespoons olive oil
1–2 cloves garlic crushed
1 medium onion, sliced
2 slices bacon
4–5 cups brown or vegetable stock
1 stalk celery, finely sliced
1 leek, white part only cut into match-like shreds
2 small carrots, shredded
½ cup chopped cabbage
1–2 small zucchini, cut in strips
¾ cup tomatoes, canned or fresh
1 teaspoon tomato purée
6–7 green beans, chopped
2–3 tablespoons peas
½ cup macaroni, broken into pieces
2 tablespoons chopped mixed parsley, marjoram, oregano, and basil

GARNISH
1 cup grated Parmesan (or other hard cheese)

1. Soak the beans overnight in cold water. Then drain and put them in a pan with 2 cups slightly salted water. Put the lid on the pan, and bring to a boil. Then simmer for 2 hours until tender.

2. In another pan heat the oil, and cook the garlic, onion and diced bacon until golden brown. Add to the bean pot, with the stock, celery, leek, and carrots. Cook together for 20 minutes. Then add finely sliced cabbage, zucchini, chopped tomatoes, tomato purée, green beans, peas, macaroni and chopped herbs. Cook for 15–20 minutes more.

3. Season to taste, and serve with plenty of grated cheese in a separate bowl.

Soupe au Pistou

4 tablespoons butter
1 large onion or 3 leeks, sliced
3 potatoes, sliced
2–3 large ripe tomatoes, peeled and chopped (or ¾ cup canned tomatoes)
6–7 cups stock
chopped parsley
a pinch of oregano
1 cup sliced green beans
2–3 tablespoons vermicelli
2–3 cloves garlic
several sprigs of fresh basil (or 2 teaspoons dried basil)
2 slices tomato, grilled or fried

GARNISH
grated cheese

A type of minestrone, but with the addition of garlic, which gives a strong and unmistakable taste. (Serves 6–8 hot)

1. Melt the butter, and cook the onion or leeks and potatoes for 5–6 minutes without browning. Add the tomatoes. Pour on stock and bring to a boil. Add herbs, seasoning, beans and vermicelli. Cook over a low heat until all are tender.

2. Meanwhile prepare a garlic paste: Crush the garlic and mix with the basil and 2 slices of grilled or fried tomato. Pound all together to make a smooth paste, adding a little of the juice from the soup to moisten.

3. Add this mixture to the soup just before serving and mix well. Serve hot, with grated cheese in a separate dish.

Green Pea Soup

2 tablespoons butter
1 small onion (or several young green onions) finely chopped
1 head of lettuce, washed and sliced
2 cups fresh or frozen peas
4 cups chicken stock
sugar to taste
1 sprig of mint (or 1 teaspoon dried mint)

GARNISH
4–6 tablespoons heavy cream
2 teaspoons fresh (or dried chopped) mint
fried bread or bacon croutons (see garnish section)

Creamy pea soup delicately flavored with a touch of mint (Serves 4–6, hot)

1. Melt the butter and soften the onion and lettuce for 4–5 minutes without browning.

2. Measure 2 cups of peas, and add 1½ cups to the soup pan, reserving the remainder as garnish. Add stock, salt, pepper, sugar to taste, and mint. Cover pan with lid and cook gently until tender, about 20 minutes.

3. Put soup into electric blender, first removing mint stalk, and blend until smooth; or put through food mill or fine sieve.

4. Meanwhile, cook the remaining peas in a little boiling salted and sugared water. Drain and divide among soup cups.

5. Re-heat the soup, and adjust seasoning to taste. Pour into soup cups, add a tablespoon of cream to each cup, sprinkle with chopped mint and serve with fried bread croutons or bacon croutons (see garnish section).

Purée of Turnip Soup

2 cups sliced young turnips
1 cup sliced potatoes
1 small onion, sliced
3 tablespoons butter
1½ tablespoons flour
3 cups white or chicken stock
1 cup milk
1 tablespoon chopped parsley (or 1 teaspoon paprika)

GARNISH
bacon croutons (see garnish section)

Turnips and potatoes cooked in butter and puréed with white stock (Serves 4–6, hot)

1. Melt the butter and cook the turnips, potatoes and onion gently until they are tender, 20–30 minutes. Sprinkle in a little flour and blend thoroughly. Pour on the stock and mix well before bringing to a boil. Reduce the heat and simmer for 15 minutes.

2. Put soup into the electric blender and blend until smooth. Re-heat, adding more seasoning, if necessary, and the milk.

3. Sprinkle with parsley or paprika on top, and serve bacon croutons separately.

Creole Soup

3 tablespoons butter, oil or bacon fat
½ cup chopped green and red peppers
1 onion, chopped
2 tablespoons flour
2 teaspoons tomato purée
4 large ripe tomatoes (or ¾ cup canned tomatoes)
4 cups stock
1 bay leaf, 4 sprigs of parsley, 1 sprig of thyme, tied together
a pinch of cayenne pepper
¼ teaspoon paprika pepper
¼ teaspoon sugar
1 teaspoon vinegar
2–3 teaspoons grated fresh horseradish (or 1 teaspoon dried horseradish)

GARNISH
1 tablespoon chopped parsley
garlic croutons (see garnish section)

A spicy tomato and pepper soup, suitable for winter meals (Serves 4, hot—see picture, p. 6)

1. Melt butter, oil or bacon fat. Cook the peppers and onions gently for 5–6 minutes without browning. Stir in flour and blend well; add tomato purée, chopped, de-seeded fresh or canned tomatoes, stock, bay leaf, herbs and seasoning. Bring to a boil, stirring constantly. Then reduce heat and simmer for 25–30 minutes.

2. Remove the bay leaf and herbs, and adjust seasoning. Add freshly grated or dried horseradish and vinegar. If soup is not a good enough color a little more tomato purée can now be added. Serve hot, sprinkled with chopped herbs and garlic croutons.

Pea Hull Soup

4–5 handsful of young pea hulls
1 medium onion (or 3–4 shallots) finely chopped
4–5 cups chicken or veal stock (or cubes and water)
3–4 sprigs of parsley (or 1 tablespoon dried parsley)
1 sprig of fresh mint (or 2–3 pinches of dry mint)
2 tablespoons butter
1½ tablespoons flour
sugar to taste

GARNISH
4–6 tablespoons whipped cream
1 tablespoon finely chopped mint

An unusual soup made from young tender pea hulls, which can be served hot or chilled (Serves 4–6)

1. Shell peas and wash hulls, reserving peas for future use. Put hulls into a pan with the onion, stock, parsley and mint. Bring to a boil and simmer until tender, about 20 minutes. Then press the pulp from the pea hulls through a nylon sieve or food mill.

2. Melt butter, and blend in the flour. Add the purée from hulls and then the liquid in which they were cooked. Blend carefully. Bring to a boil, and add salt, pepper and sugar to taste.

3. Serve hot or chilled with a spoonful of whipped cream on top of each cup and sprinkled with chopped parsley.

Potage Solferino

3 leeks, sliced
2 small young carrots, thinly sliced
2 medium potatoes, peeled and sliced
3 tablespoons butter
1 small clove garlic crushed (or shake of garlic powder)
4 ripe tomatoes (or ½ cup canned tomatoes)
1 tablespoon chopped parsley
¼ teaspoon chopped basil
½ bay leaf
½ teaspoon sugar
4–5 cups stock or water
2 teaspoons tomato purée

GARNISH
1 ripe tomato, peeled, seeded and chopped (or 3–4 tablespoons potato dice cooked in boiling salted water)
1 tablespoon chopped parsley

A delicious tomato and vegetable soup (Serves 4–6, hot)

1. Melt the butter and cook the leeks, carrots and potatoes gently for 5–6 minutes, stirring constantly to prevent browning. Add the garlic.

2. If using fresh tomatoes, dip them into boiling water for 10 seconds, then into cold. Peel and chop, and add to soup with herbs and seasoning. Pour on stock or water, and bring soup to a boil. Then reduce heat and simmer for 20–30 minutes or until the vegetables are tender. Remove bay leaf.

3. Put soup through a fine food mill or electric blender, and blend until smooth. Re-heat, adding the tomato purée, and adjust seasoning to taste.

4. Serve hot, garnished with the chopped flesh of one peeled and seeded tomato or potato dice cooked in a little boiling water. Sprinkle with chopped parsley.

French Onion Soup

Strongly-flavored brown onion soup, garnished with French bread and cheese, and browned in the oven or broiler (Serves 4–6, hot)

3–4 tablespoons butter
4–5 medium onions, peeled and finely sliced
1–2 cloves garlic, crushed
½ teaspoon sugar
2 tablespoons flour
5 cups vegetable stock (or water)
½ cup white wine (optional)
1 bay leaf
3–4 sprigs of parsley
1 sprig of thyme
a pinch of nutmeg
4–6 slices French bread (long flute or yard of bread type)
4–6 tablespoons grated mixed Gruyere or Emmentaler and Parmesan cheese or other strong hard cheese

1. Melt the butter, and add the onions and garlic and a sprinkling of sugar. Brown slowly, stirring constantly to prevent burning. Sprinkle in the flour and brown this slightly. Add the stock or water, and the wine if using any—otherwise add the equivalent amount of water. Bring to a boil, stirring constantly. Add herbs and seasoning, and simmer for 20–30 minutes.

2. Meanwhile, cut the French bread into slices and put into the oven to dry and brown slightly.

3. Remove bay leaf from soup. Put the slices of bread into the oven-proof soup bowls or a large tureen. Pour the soup over the bread, sprinkle thickly with cheese and put into a hot oven for 15–20 minutes or under broiler for 7–10 minutes to brown the cheese.

Spinach Soup

- 4–5 handsful fresh spinach (or 1 package frozen spinach)
- 3 tablespoons butter
- 1 onion, finely chopped
- 1½ tablespoons flour
- 4 cups white or vegetable stock (or water and chicken cube)
- 3–4 sprigs of parsley (or 1 tablespoon dried parsley)
- 1 bay leaf
- a squeeze or two of lemon juice
- ¼–½ teaspoon powdered mace
- ½ cup cream

GARNISH
- 2 hard-boiled eggs, sliced
- paprika
- or
- fried bread croutons or bacon croutons (see garnish section)

A quickly made spinach soup garnished with hard-boiled egg slices (Serves 4–6, hot)

1. Wash the spinach thoroughly if using fresh spinach, drain and shake off excess water. Melt butter, and cook the onion and spinach gently until the spinach has softened and become limp, without browning. If using frozen spinach allow block to unfreeze completely during this process. Sprinkle in flour and blend smoothly. Add the stock (or water and cubes). Bring soup to a boil, stirring constantly. Then add parsley, bay leaf and seasoning. Reduce heat and simmer for 10–12 minutes. Do not overcook as this spoils the green color and fresh flavor.

2. Put soup through a fine food mill, or blend until smooth in an electric blender. Re-heat, adding a little lemon juice. Adjust seasoning and add the mace. Stir in the cream just before serving.

3. Garnish with slices of hard-boiled egg in each cup sprinkled with paprika, or alternatively with fried bread or bacon croutons.

Watercress Soup

A creamy green watercress soup garnished with watercress sprigs and croutons (Serves 4–6, hot)

2 bunches fresh watercress
3 tablespoons butter
1 potato, sliced
1 small onion, finely chopped
1 tablespoon flour
3 cups white or chicken stock (or water)
3–4 sprigs of parsley
1 bay leaf
2 cups milk
¼ teaspoon mace
a little green coloring (optional)

GARNISH
watercress sprigs
4–6 tablespoons cream
fried bread croutons (see garnish section)

1. Wash and pick over the watercress, discarding any yellow leaves. Reserve enough green top-sprigs to make the final garnish, and chop the remaining cress roughly. Melt the butter and cook the potato and onion together for 2–3 minutes before adding the chopped watercress. Continue cooking for 3–4 minutes, stirring constantly to prevent browning. Sprinkle in flour and blend well. Add stock and blend together before bringing to a boil. Add herbs and some seasoning, reduce heat, and simmer until the potato is tender, about 20 minutes.

2. Remove bay leaf. Put soup into electric blender and blend until smooth, or put through fine food mill or sieve. Return soup to pan and re-heat gently. At the same time heat milk in a separate pan. When almost at boiling point, pour into watercress mixture—this makes texture of soup lighter and more delicate. Adjust seasoning, adding mace and a little green coloring if desired.

3. Serve with a spoon of cream in each cup and the reserved watercress sprigs on top. Fried bread croutons are also excellent with this soup.

French Tomato Soup

2 large onions, finely sliced
2 slices of bacon, chopped
1 tablespoon butter
4–6 ripe tomatoes (or 1 cup canned tomatoes) chopped
1 tablespoon tomato purée
2–3 strips of lemon rind
4 cups chicken stock
1 teaspoon sugar
1 tablespoon parsley
¼ teaspoon thyme
1 teaspoon basil

GARNISH
1 tablespoon chopped mixed parsley and basil
fried garlic croutons (see garnish section)

Tomato soup flavored with bacon, lemon and herbs, and served with garlic croutons—a winter soup (Serves 4–6, hot)

1. Heat the bacon pieces in a pan. When the fat has run, add the butter. When it has melted, add the onions and cook gently for 5–6 minutes until tender and golden brown. Add the tomatoes and tomato purée, lemon rind, stock, salt, pepper, sugar and herbs. Bring to a boil. Then simmer for 20 minutes or until tomatoes are tender.

2. Put soup through a food mill or blend in electric blender. Adjust seasoning and serve hot, sprinkled with chopped parsley and basil and with fried garlic croutons.

Russian Sauerkraut Soup

1 onion, sliced
2 small carrots, sliced
3–4 tablespoons butter
1 potato, peeled and sliced
2 tablespoons flour
1 teaspoon tomato purée
¾ lb sauerkraut
4–5 cups brown or household stock
1 tablespoon chopped parsley
1 teaspoon chopped chervil

GARNISH
sour cream

Strongly flavored Russian soup containing sauerkraut and garnished with sour cream (Serves 4–6, hot)

1. Melt the butter, and cook the onion and carrots until golden. Then add the potato. Stir in flour, and when smooth, add the tomato purée and sauerkraut. Cook for a few minutes, stirring constantly. Then add the stock and the herbs.

2. Bring to a boil, and simmer for about 40 minutes. Season to taste, and serve hot with a spoonful of sour cream in each soup cup.

Cauliflower Soup

A white soup flavored with cauliflower and sprinkled with cheese (Serves 4–6, hot)

1 medium cauliflower
1 bay leaf
1 onion, chopped
1 medium potato, sliced
3 tablespoons butter
1 tablespoon flour
5 cups milk
½ cup cream
¼ teaspoon mace

GARNISH
1 tablespoon chopped chervil
grated cheese

1. Divide well washed cauliflower into flowerets, and cut the hard stalk and leaves into small pieces. Cook the cauliflower in boiling salted water with bay leaf for 4–5 minutes to lightly cook and to remove any strong flavor. Drain and rinse under cold water. Reserve ½–¾ cup of small flowerets for garnish.

2. Meanwhile, melt the butter, add the onion and potato, and cook gently for 5–6 minutes, stirring to prevent browning. Sprinkle in flour, and blend smoothly. Then pour in milk, and mix well before bringing to a boil. Add the cauliflower, then reduce heat, and simmer gently until potatoes and cauliflower are just tender.

3. Put the soup into an electric blender and blend until smooth, or put through a fine food mill. Return to pan and re-heat, adding the reserved cauliflower flowerets. Add seasoning and the cream.

4. Sprinkle with chopped chervil and serve grated cheese separately.

Leek and Potato Soup

Leeks and potatoes blended into a creamy soup (Serves 4–6, hot)

4 leeks
2 medium potatoes
3–4 tablespoons butter
2 tablespoons flour
4 cups white, chicken or vegetable stock (or water and cubes)
3–4 sprigs of parsley
1 bay leaf
¼ teaspoon grated nutmeg (or powdered mace)
1 cup creamy milk

GARNISH
½ tablespoon chopped chives (or 1 tablespoon chopped parsley)
cheese croutons (see garnish section)

1. Slice the white parts of the leeks and wash well in salted cold water. Peel and slice the potatoes finely. Melt the butter and add the potato and drained leeks. Cook gently for 5–6 minutes, stirring to prevent sticking and browning. Sprinkle in flour. When thoroughly mixed, add stock (or water and cubes). Add herbs and seasoning. Bring to a boil, stirring constantly. Then lower heat, and simmer for 25–30 minutes or until vegetables are tender.

2. Blend the soup in an electric blender or put through a fine food mill. Re-heat and adjust seasoning. Put the milk into a separate pan, and bring to just below boiling point before adding it to the soup.

3. Sprinkle with chives or chopped parsley in each soup cup, and serve cheese croutons separately.

Chervil Soup

An interesting and unusually flavored soup, liked by devotees of herbs (Serves 4–6, hot)

2 young carrots, finely sliced
1 small potato, finely sliced
4–5 cups chicken or white stock
3 sprigs of parsley
3 tablespoons butter
2 tablespoons flour
¼ teaspoon mace or a pinch of nutmeg
¼ cup chopped fresh chervil
½ cup cream

GARNISH
fried bread croutons (see garnish section)

1. Put carrots and potato in a pan with stock and parsley sprigs, and simmer until tender, 15–20 minutes.

2. Melt butter and stir in flour. When smooth, strain stock on to flour and butter, and mix well.

3. Blend the potato and carrots in electric blender and add to soup. Mix well. Then bring to a boil, stirring constantly. Simmer for a few minutes, adding salt, pepper and mace or nutmeg.

4. Just before serving add the chopped chervil and cream. Re-heat but do not boil, as this destroys the delicate flavor of chervil.

5. Serve with fried bread croutons.

Lettuce Soup

Light summery soup, suitable to serve either hot with croutons or cold (Serves 4–6, hot or cold)

2–3 heads lettuce
3 tablespoons butter
1 small onion or 6–8 young green onions, finely chopped
2 tablespoons flour
4 cups chicken stock (or water and cubes)
½ teaspoon sugar
3–4 sprigs of parsley (or 1 tablespoon dried parsley)
2 sprigs of mint (or 1 teaspoon chopped mint)
1 cup creamy milk

GARNISH
4–6 tablespoons heavy cream
2 teaspoons finely chopped mint or parsley
fried bread croutons (or brown bread and butter)

1. Chop the well washed lettuces coarsely. Melt butter and soften the lettuce and onion gently in a covered pan for 5–6 minutes without browning. Sprinkle in the flour and blend smoothly before adding the stock and seasoning. When smooth, bring to a boil, stirring constantly. Reduce heat and simmer for 15 minutes, having added salt, pepper, sugar, parsley and mint.

2. Put soup into electric blender and blend until smooth, or put through food mill or fine sieve.

3. Re-heat soup in clean pan. Meanwhile, heat the creamy milk in another pan and add when on the point of boiling–this lightens the texture of the soup. Adjust seasoning to taste.

4. If serving hot, pour into soup cups and put a large spoonful of cream on top of each cup. Sprinkle with chopped parsley or mint. If serving cold, chill thoroughly, adding a little more seasoning. Serve in soup cups with a spoon of whipped heavy cream on top, and sprinkle with chopped herbs as above.

5. If serving hot serve with fried bread croutons; if cold, with brown bread and butter.

Parsley Soup

A nourishing and deliciously different green soup (Serves 4–6, hot)

2½ cups fresh chopped parsley
3 tablespoons butter
1 onion, chopped
1 stalk celery, chopped
2 tablespoons flour
5 cups vegetable or white stock
a pinch of nutmeg
½ bay leaf

GARNISH
4–6 tablespoons heavy cream
a sprinkling of paprika
fried bread or bacon croutons (see garnish section)

1. Coarsely chop the parsley including the stems, which are full of flavor.

2. Melt the butter, and cook the onion and celery gently for a few minutes without browning. Sprinkle in flour and mix well. Pour on stock and bring slowly to a boil, blending smoothly. Add the chopped parsley and salt, pepper, nutmeg and bay leaf. Simmer for 25 minutes.

3. The soup can be served as it is, blended in an electric blender or put through a food mill.

4. Re-heat soup, pour into soup bowls and serve with a spoonful of cream in each bowl, a sprinkling of paprika, and fried bread or bacon croutons.

Parsnip Soup

An unusual soup, popular with those who like the rather sweet taste of parsnips (Serves 4, hot)

3 tablespoons butter
1½ cups peeled and finely sliced parsnips
1 onion, chopped
1 tablespoon flour
3–4 cups vegetable or white stock (or water and cube)
3–4 sprigs of parsley
1 small bay leaf
a pinch of thyme
a pinch of nutmeg
½ cup cream

GARNISH
1 tablespoon chopped parsley
fried bread croutons (see garnish section)

1. Melt the butter, and cook the onion and parsnips gently for 5–6 minutes with a lid on the pan, to soften without browning. Remove from heat, and sprinkle in flour. Then blend well. Pour on stock, mix well, and add herbs and seasonings. Bring to a boil, and simmer for 20–30 minutes until the parsnips are tender. Remove bay leaf.

2. Put soup into electric blender, and blend until smooth, or put through food mill. Return soup to pan, adjust seasoning and re-heat, adding cream.

3. Serve in soup cups sprinkled with chopped parsley and with fried bread croutons.

Green Bean Soup

Delicious and unusual light soup of green beans (Serves 4–6, hot)

2–3 tablespoons butter
1 medium onion (or 3–4 shallots) finely chopped
1 clove garlic, crushed
2 tablespoons flour
4 cups chicken or veal stock
1 pound green beans
1 teaspoon chopped or dried summer savory
a little green coloring if required

GARNISH
4–6 tablespoons whipping cream
2 slices bacon

1. Melt the butter and cook the onion and garlic for 5–6 minutes in a covered pan. Add the flour and blend in smoothly. Pour on stock and mix well. When smooth, bring to a boil, stirring constantly. Add salt and pepper.

2. String the beans and cut in slanting slices or break in half depending on their size. Add to the soup, with dried savory, and cook for 25 minutes or until beans are tender.

3. Strain the soup, reserving a few pieces of bean for garnish (keep warm). Put remaining soup and beans through a food mill or blend until smooth in electric blender.

4. Re-heat soup, adjust seasoning to taste and add a little green coloring if required.

5. Serve hot with a spoon of whipped cream on each cup, and sprinkled with finely crumbled crispy fried bacon.

4 CREAM SOUPS

Cream of Asparagus Soup

The Queen of cream soups, whether made from green or white asparagus (Serves 4, hot)

1 pound asparagus, green or white (or equivalent amount of canned asparagus)
1 onion, finely chopped
3–4 sprigs of parsley
3–4 cups chicken stock (or water and chicken stock cubes)
3 tablespoons butter
2 tablespoons flour
¼ teaspoon mace
a little green coloring, if necessary

LIAISON
2 egg yolks
½ cup heavy cream

GARNISH
fried bread croutons (see garnish section)

1. If using fresh asparagus, wash, scrape and trim it. Remove tips for garnish. If using canned asparagus, merely remove tips and drain off liquid, reserving it for making soup.

2. Chop the asparagus stalks and put in a pot with chopped onion. Add parsley sprigs, 3–4 cups of chicken stock (or water and chicken cubes), and the liquid from can if canned asparagus is used. Add a little salt and pepper. Cover pan with lid and simmer for 10–15 minutes or until the asparagus is tender.

3. Put into electric blender and blend until smooth, or through food mill or fine nylon sieve.

4. Melt butter and add the flour. Stir until smooth, and cook for a minute or two. Remove from heat and strain into the asparagus soup. Blend smoothly, bring to a boil, stirring constantly, and simmer for a few minutes. Adjust seasoning to taste, and add some mace.

5. Meanwhile, in a small pan cook the reserved tips for about 5–7 minutes in a little hot stock or water, until tender. Strain liquid into soup and divide tips into soup cups equally.

6. Make liaison: Mix egg yolks and cream well. Add a few spoonfuls of hot soup and mix well before straining into soup, stirring constantly. Re-heat soup gently without allowing it to boil.

7. If soup is not a good color, a little green coloring can be added, but great care must be exercised as it can easily be overdone. Serve soup hot with fried bread croutons.

Cream of Mushroom Soup

4 tablespoons butter
1 onion, chopped
2–3 cups sliced mushrooms
3 tablespoons flour
3 cups chicken or white stock (or water and cube)
1 bay leaf
3–4 sprigs of parsley
¼ teaspoon mace
2 cups creamy milk

GARNISH
chopped parsley or chives
fried bread croutons (see garnish section)

Creamy mushroom-flavored soup (Serves 4–6, hot)

1. Melt the butter and cook the onion for 4–5 minutes to soften. Then add the mushrooms, cover pan and cook for 5 more minutes. Sprinkle in the flour, and stir until smooth. Pour on the stock, and mix well. Add bay leaf, parsley and mace. Season with salt and pepper. Bring to a boil, and simmer for 10–15 minutes.

2. Remove bay leaf. Put soup through a fine food mill or into an electric blender and blend until smooth. Re-heat, adding the heated milk. Adjust seasoning to taste.

3. Sprinkle with chopped parsley or chives, and serve with fried bread croutons.

Cream of Tomato Soup

3 tablespoons butter
1 large onion, chopped
1 carrot, chopped
1 stalk celery, sliced (or 1 teaspoon dried celery)
2 tablespoons flour
1 tablespoon tomato purée
1 pound of fresh ripe tomatoes (or 1½ cups canned tomatoes)
1½ cups vegetable stock (or chicken stock)
1 teaspoon sugar
¼ teaspoon paprika
1 bay leaf
3–4 sprigs of parsley
a sprig (or a good pinch) of thyme
2½ cups milk

GARNISH
4–6 tablespoons heavy cream (or sour cream, if desired)
1 tablespoon chopped parsley (or chives)
cheesy croutons (see garnish section)

A fairly thick, creamy tomato soup served with cheesy croutons (Serves 4–6, hot)

1. Melt the butter and cook the onion, carrot and celery gently for 5–6 minutes to soften without browning, stirring frequently. Sprinkle in the flour, and mix well. Then stir in the tomato purée and the chopped tomatoes. Add the stock, and the sugar, salt, pepper, paprika and herbs. Bring to a boil, stirring constantly. Reduce heat, and simmer for about 30 minutes. Remove the bay leaf.

2. Put the soup through a fine food mill, or blend until smooth in an electric blender. Re-heat soup. In a separate pan heat the milk to just below boiling point and add to the soup mixing thoroughly. Adjust seasoning to taste.

3. Serve with a spoonful of cream on top of each soup cup, a sprinkling of herbs, and cheesy croutons.

Cream of Curry Soup

3 tablespoons butter
1 large onion, chopped
1 sour cooking apple, peeled and cored
½ tablespoon curry powder or paste (or more if desired)
1 tablespoon flour
2 tablespoons rice
4–5 cups chicken stock (or water and cubes)
1 teaspoon sweet chutney
2 teaspoons coconut
1 bay leaf
3–4 sprigs of parsley
1 slice lemon
½ cup cream

GARNISH
1 tablespoon chopped parsley (or paprika)
lemon wedges
½–1 cup plain boiled rice

Creamy soup with a delicious curry flavor (Serves 4–6, hot)

1. Melt the butter, and cook the onion and apple gently for 5–6 minutes to soften without browning. Stir in curry powder or paste and cook for 1 minute. Remove from heat and sprinkle in flour. Blend well. Then add rice, stock, chutney and coconut. Bring to a boil, stirring constantly. Reduce heat. Add seasonings, herbs and slice of lemon. Cover pan, and simmer for 15–20 minutes to cook the rice.

2. Remove bay leaf and lemon. Put soup into electric blender and blend until smooth. Re-heat, adjust seasoning, and just before serving stir in cream.

3. Sprinkle with chopped parsley or paprika, and serve lemon wedges and plain boiled rice separately.

Cream of Corn Soup

Creamy potato and corn soup sprinkled with chives or parsley (Serves 4–6, hot)

3 tablespoons butter
1 onion, chopped
1 medium potato, finely sliced
1½ cups fresh or canned corn
3½ cups milk
1 bay leaf
3–4 sprigs of parsley
¼ teaspoon mace
1 chicken stock cube

GARNISH
4–6 spoons heavy cream
1 tablespoon chopped chives or parsley (or a sprinkling of paprika)
fried bread croutons (see garnish section)

1. Melt the butter, and cook the onion and potato gently with a lid on the pan for 5 minutes, shaking the pan occasionally to prevent sticking. Add 1 cup of the corn. Stir well. Then add the milk, bay leaf, parsley, salt, pepper and mace. Bring to simmering heat, add a chicken stock cube and cook until vegetables are tender.

2. Put soup into electric blender and blend until smooth, or put through fine food mill.

3. Return soup to the pan with the remaining corn (which if fresh should be simmered until tender in salted water). Re-heat soup until nearly boiling, and adjust seasoning.

4. Serve in soup cups with a spoonful of cream in each cup, a sprinkling of chopped chives, parsley or paprika, and fried bread croutons.

Curried Corn Soup

Made in the same way as Cream of Corn Soup, but with curry flavoring (Serves 4–6, hot)

1. Using the recipe for cream of Corn Soup (see above) add 2 teaspoons of curry powder to the onion and potato mixture, and cook with those ingredients. If using canned corn use mixed corn and pimento rather than the plain corn.

2. Garnish the soup with paprika.

Cream of Carrot Soup

4 tablespoons butter
1½ cups sliced young carrots
1 large onion, finely sliced
½ clove garlic
2 tablespoons rice
3–4 sprigs of parsley (or 1 tablespoon dried parsley)
thinly peeled rind from ½ orange
4 cups chicken or white stock
¼ teaspoon sugar
juice of ½ orange

LIAISON
2 egg yolks
¼ cup cream

GARNISH
finely grated rind of ½ orange
2 teaspoons chopped parsley

Delicious orange-colored soup with delicate flavor of carrot and orange (Serves 4–6, hot)

1. Melt the butter and add vegetables, crushed garlic and rice. Mix well over gentle heat for 5 minutes without browning. Add the parsley, orange rind, stock, sugar and seasonings. Bring soup to a boil. Then lower heat, and simmer for 30–40 minutes, or until vegetables are tender.

2. Put soup into electric blender and blend until smooth, or put through food mill. Return to pot, and re-heat, adding orange juice.

3. If soup is not thick enough, add cream and egg yolk liaison: Mix the egg yolks and cream well. Put a few spoons of hot soup into the liaison. Then strain back into soup, stirring constantly. Re-heat soup without allowing to boil.

4. Serve in soup cups, sprinkled with grated orange rind and parsley.

Almond Cream Soup

A very delicately flavored almond and chicken soup (Serves 4, hot or cold)

1 small potato, finely sliced
3–4 spring onions, finely sliced (or 2–3 slices of ordinary onion)
3–4 stalks celery, finely sliced
3 cups chicken or white stock
½–¾ cup almonds
1 small bay leaf
3–4 sprigs of parsley
2 tablespoons butter
1 tablespoon flour
a pinch of mace
4–5 tablespoons heavy cream

1. Put the potato, onions and celery in a pan with the stock, bay leaf and sprigs of parsley. Simmer gently with lid on until the potato slices are tender.

2. Meanwhile, pour boiling water on to the almonds, let stand for a few minutes, then drain and pop almonds out of their skins. Reserve 10–12 whole almonds for garnish, and chop or finely grind the remainder. This can be done in an electric blender but a little stock should be added to liquify slightly. Add this paste to the pan, and cook for another 20 minutes.

3. Remove the bay leaf and sprigs of parsley. Pour soup into the electric blender and blend slowly until smooth. Strain through a fine sieve.

4. Melt the butter, add the flour and stir until smooth off the heat. Add the strained soup slowly, stirring until smooth. Bring to a boil, stirring constantly. Add salt, pepper and mace, being careful not to overpower the light almond flavor.

5. Cut the remaining almonds into slivers, brown lightly in a cool oven, and sprinkle with a little salt.

6. Add a spoonful of cream to each soup cup, and at the last moment sprinkle with the crisp brown almonds. The soup can also be served chilled.

Cream of Celery Soup

1 slice bacon
3–4 tablespoons butter
2 cups chopped celery or celeriac
1 large onion, chopped
1 potato, sliced
1 tablespoon flour
2 cups water (or white stock)
1 bay leaf
several sprigs of parsley
a pinch of thyme
3 cups milk

GARNISH
4–6 tablespoons cream
paprika
fried bread croutons or bacon croutons (see garnish section)

Creamy celery and potato soup garnished with croutons or bacon croutons (Serves 4–6, hot)

1. Chop the bacon and put in a pan with the butter. Cook gently for a few minutes. Then add the celery, potato and onion. Cook together for 4–5 minutes, stirring constantly to prevent browning. Sprinkle in the flour and blend smoothly. Add the stock or water, mix well, and bring to a boil. Reduce the heat, add bay leaf, parsley sprigs and thyme. Simmer for 20–30 minutes, or until the vegetables are tender.

2. Put soup through fine food mill or into electric blender and blend until smooth. Re-heat gently. In another pan heat the milk, and when nearly boiling add to soup pan with seasoning to taste.

3. Serve with a spoon of cream and a dusting of paprika in each soup cup, and fried bread croutons or bacon croutons separately.

Cream of Potato Soup

A creamy potato and onion soup made with milk (Serves 4–6, hot)

- 3 tablespoons butter
- 3–4 medium potatoes, finely sliced
- 2 medium onions, finely sliced
- 1–2 stalks celery, finely sliced
- 2½ cups boiling water
- 1 bay leaf
- 3–4 sprigs of parsley
- a pinch of thyme
- ¼ teaspoon mace or nutmeg
- 2 cups milk

GARNISH

- 4–6 tablespoons heavy cream
- 1 tablespoon chopped chives or parsley
- fried bread croutons or cheesy croutons (see garnish section)

1. Melt the butter and cook the potatoes, onions and celery very gently, stirring frequently, without allowing them to brown, for about 5–6 minutes. Add the boiling water and stir well. Add herbs, salt and pepper, mace or nutmeg. Bring to a boil. Then reduce heat, and simmer gently with lid on pan for about 30–40 minutes, or until the vegetables are tender. Stir from time to time to keep vegetables from sticking and browning.

2. Remove bay leaf. Then put soup through fine food mill or into electric blender, and blend until smooth. Re-heat. Then add the milk which has been heated until nearly boiling in a separate pan—this lightens the texture of the soup. Adjust seasoning.

3. Serve with a spoon of cream in each cup, a sprinkling of chopped chives or parsley, and fried bread croutons or cheesy croutons.

Cream of Brussel Sprout Soup

An unusual green winter soup with a delicious nutty flavor (Serves 4–6, hot)

- 4 tablespoons butter
- 1 onion, chopped
- 1 potato, chopped
- 4 cups washed and trimmed Brussel sprouts, chopped
- 1½ tablespoons flour
- 4 cups white stock (or water and chicken cubes)
- 2 bay leaves
- 3–4 sprigs of parsley
- ¼ teaspoon mace
- 1 cup light cream or milk

GARNISH

- 1 cup of cooked chestnuts, broken into pieces
- 2–3 tablespoons butter
- seasoning

1. Melt the butter, and cook the onion and potato for 2–3 minutes. Then add the chopped sprouts, and cook for a further 5 minutes, stirring constantly. Sprinkle in the flour and blend well. Then pour on stock. Stir until well mixed and smooth. Then bring to a boil, stirring constantly. Reduce the heat, add the bay leaves, parsley sprigs and seasoning. Cover and simmer soup for about 20 minutes, or until vegetables are tender; but not overcooked, as this would give the soup an unpleasant flavor.

2. Remove bay leaves. Then put the soup through a food mill, or into an electric blender and blend until smooth. Adjust seasoning, and re-heat soup, adding at the last moment a cup of hot cream or creamy milk.

3. Sprinkle with pieces of cooked chestnut, fried in butter until golden brown.

Cream of Chicken Soup

Creamy chicken-flavored soup enriched with egg yolks and cream, and garnished with cooked chopped chicken (Serves 4–6, hot)

- 1 small onion, chopped
- 2 stalks celery, sliced
- 4–5 button mushrooms, sliced
- 3 tablespoons butter
- 2 tablespoons flour
- 4–5 cups well-flavored chicken stock
- 1 small bay leaf, 2–3 sprigs of parsley tied together
- ¼ teaspoon mace
- ¼–½ cup chopped cooked white chicken meat

LIAISON

- 2 egg yolks
- ½ cup cream

GARNISH

- 1 tablespoon chopped tarragon or 2 tablespoons chopped parsley

1. Melt the butter, and cook the onion, celery and mushrooms gently with lid on for 5–6 minutes without allowing to brown. Sprinkle in flour, and mix well. Pour in stock, and blend until smooth. Bring soup to a boil, stirring constantly, and then reduce heat. Add the herbs and seasoning. Simmer gently for 20–30 minutes.

2. Remove herbs and put soup through a fine food mill or blend until smooth in an electric blender. Return soup to pan and re-heat, adding the chopped chicken meat. Adjust seasoning.

3. Make the egg and cream liaison: Mix the egg yolks and cream together thoroughly. Add a few spoonfuls of hot soup to this. Mix thoroughly, and then strain back into the soup, stirring constantly. Do not allow the soup to boil or the egg will curdle.

4. Serve hot in soup cups sprinkled with chopped parsley or tarragon.

Cream of Artichoke Soup

A creamy, warming winter soup, delicately flavored with Jerusalem artichokes, and served with crisp golden fried croutons (Serves 4–6, hot)

2 cups water
1 teaspoon lemon juice
1 bay leaf
3–4 sprigs of parsley
1 teaspoon salt
pepper and mace to taste
3 cups peeled and sliced Jerusalem artichokes
3 tablespoons butter
1 onion, finely sliced
1 stalk celery, finely sliced
2 tablespoons flour
2 cups milk

LIAISON
2 egg yolks
½ cup cream

GARNISH
1 tablespoon chopped parsley
fried bread croutons (see garnish section)

1. Put the water, lemon juice, bay leaf, parsley sprigs and seasoning into a pan and add the finely sliced artichokes. Bring to a boil, and simmer until tender, about 10–15 minutes.

2. Melt the butter and cook the finely sliced onion and celery slowly with lid on pan until soft. Do not allow to brown. Sprinkle in flour, and blend well.

3. When artichokes are tender strain the liquid on to the onion mixture and blend well. Remove bay leaf and parsley sprigs, and add these to soup. Mix in artichokes, and bring to a boil, stirring constantly. Put soup through a food grinder or fine sieve, or blend thoroughly in an electric blender until creamy.

4. Return to pan and re-heat. At the same time, in another pan heat the milk to just below boiling point. Pour into artichoke soup and whisk together (adding hot rather than cold milk makes the soup lighter and more delicate).

5. Make the liaison, by mixing the egg yolks and cream thoroughly. Add a few spoonfuls of hot soup, mix well; then strain the liaison into soup, stirring constantly.

6. Re-heat soup, being careful not to boil it or the egg will curdle. Sprinkle with chopped parsley and serve with fried bread croutons.

Cream of Chestnut Soup

A richly-flavored chestnut soup, served with fried apple-ring garnish (Serves 4–6, hot)

2–3 cups fresh peeled chestnuts (buy 2 pounds to produce this amount) or 1 large can chestnut purée (unsweetened)
3 tablespoons butter
1 large onion, sliced
2 small carrots, sliced
1 stalk celery, sliced
4–5 cups ham, chicken or brown stock (or water and bouillon cubes)
1 tablespoon chopped parsley (or 3–4 sprigs of parsley)
a pinch of thyme
1 bay leaf
a pinch of nutmeg
1 cup cream

GARNISH
2–3 cooking apples
4 tablespoons butter
1–2 teaspoon sugar
1 tablespoon chopped parsley

1. If using fresh chestnuts, prepare as follows: Make a small slit in the top of each nut and place in a well-greased pan in a moderate oven for 10–15 minutes to loosen both outer and inner skin. Remove both skins. If using canned chestnut purée, add to the soup after the vegetables have been cooked.

2. Melt the butter, and add the onion, carrots and celery. Mix well over gentle heat before adding the chestnuts. Cover the pan, and cook for 3–4 minutes, shaking the pan occasionally. Add the stock, herbs and seasoning and simmer for 20–30 minutes, or until the chestnuts and vegetables are tender.

3. Remove the bay leaf, put soup into electric blender and blend until smooth, or put through a fine food mill. Return to pan, and re-heat soup. Season to taste. Add the cream just before serving or put a spoon of cream in each soup cup.

4. Make apple-ring garnish by peeling and coring 2–3 cooking apples and cutting into rings. Melt butter and fry the apple slices until golden brown on each side, sprinkling the slices with a little sugar.

5. Float 1–2 slices of apple in each soup cup and sprinkle with chopped parsley.

Cream of Barley Soup

1 cup pearl barley
1 onion, sliced
1 carrot, sliced
2 stalks celery, sliced
1 bay leaf
3–4 sprigs of parsley (or 1 tablespoon chopped parsley)
4–5 cups chicken or veal stock
chicken carcass or ham bone, if available
½ cup cream

GARNISH
1–2 tablespoons chopped parsley
fried bacon croutons (see garnish section)

Mildly flavored creamy soup (Serves 4, hot)

1. Wash pearl barley and soak overnight if possible, otherwise cover with boiling water, and soak for 2 hours.

2. Put vegetables into pan with drained barley, herbs and stock (or cubes and water). If a chicken carcass or a ham bone is available it can be added to the soup at this stage. Cover pan with lid, and cook gently until barley is tender, about 1½–2 hours.

3. Discard bones and herbs. Then set aside the barley and strain soup through sieve, or blend soup and barley in electric blender.

4. Re-heat soup and adjust seasoning. Add the cream just before serving. Sprinkle with chopped parsley and serve with bacon-flavored croutons.

White Onion Soup

3–4 tablespoons butter
3–4 onions, finely sliced
2 tablespoons flour
4–5 cups hot milk
1 bay leaf
4 sprigs of parsley
½ teaspoon mace

LIAISON
2 egg yolks
½ cup cream

GARNISH
fried bread croutons (see garnish section)

Creamy white onion soup enriched with cream and egg yolks, a warming winter soup (Serves 4–6, hot)

1. Melt the butter and cook the onions very gently with a lid on the pan until tender, stirring frequently to prevent browning, about 10 minutes. Remove from heat and sprinkle in flour. When well mixed in, add the milk and blend well. Bring to a boil, stirring constantly. Add the bay leaf, parsley, salt, pepper and mace. Simmer soup for 15–20 minutes, stirring frequently to prevent it sticking to the bottom of the pan.

2. Make liaison: Mix the egg yolks into the cream. Add several spoonfuls of hot soup to this mixture and when blended strain back into the soup, stirring constantly. Re-heat, without boiling or the egg will curdle.

3. Serve hot with fried bread croutons.

White Vegetable Soup

1 onion or the white part of 2 leeks (well washed)
2 young carrots
2 stalks celery
3 tablespoons butter
2 tablespoons flour
4–5 cups milk
1 tablespoon chopped parsley
a pinch of dried thyme and powdered bay leaf
¼ teaspoon mace
½ cup peas (fresh or frozen)
¼ cup of green beans
¼ cup corn

LIAISON
2 egg yolks
½ cup cream

GARNISH
1 tablespoon chopped parsley
fried bread croutons (see garnish section)

A creamy soup full of tender vegetables, served with fried croutons (Serves 4–6, hot)

1. Peel and cut the root vegetables into short strips or dice. Melt the butter and cook these vegetables until tender without browning, about 5–6 minutes. Sprinkle in flour and mix well, add the milk and blend well. Slowly bring to a boil. Then reduce heat, and simmer for 10–12 minutes. Add herbs and seasoning.

2. Meanwhile, cook the peas, beans and corn in boiling salted water until just tender, 7–10 minutes. Drain and rinse under cold water. Add to the soup. Heat together for 5 minutes. Adjust seasoning and add liaison.

3. Make liaison: Mix egg yolks and cream well. Add a few spoonfuls of hot soup and stir well. Then strain back into the hot soup, stirring constantly. Re-heat soup but do not boil, or egg will curdle.

4. Serve hot in soup cups, sprinkled with chopped parsley and with fried bread croutons.

5 CHICKEN, TURKEY & GAME SOUPS

Chicken Noodle Soup

Clear chicken soup with noodles and chopped parsley (Serves 4–6, hot)

4–5 cups of well-flavored clear chicken stock (or water and cubes)
4 tablespoons fine noodles
2 tablespoons finely chopped parsley

1. Bring the stock to a boil, add the noodles, stirring constantly, and boil slowly for about 15 minutes or for time stated on package of noodles. Stir frequently to prevent noodles from sticking. Add seasoning to taste.
2. Serve hot in soup cups liberally sprinkled with finely chopped parsley.

Italian Stracciatella

Clear chicken soup with addition of beaten egg and cheese (Serves 4–6, hot)

2 large or 3 small eggs
½ cup of grated Parmesan or other hard, well-flavored cheese
5 cups well-flavored clear chicken stock
1 tablespoon chopped parsley
1 glass white wine (optional)

1. Beat the eggs well with a little salt and pepper, and stir in the grated cheese.
2. Strain the chicken stock into a pan, having removed any traces of fat. Bring to a boil, skimming if necessary, and when boiling fast pour in the cheese and egg mixture slowly with one hand, whisking the soup with the other hand. Allow the soup to continue cooking gently for a few minutes.
3. Then serve at once sprinkled with chopped parsley. A little white wine can be added to the soup if desired.

Chicken Giblet Soup

A light chicken-flavored broth garnished with cooked chicken livers and herbs. This is a good soup to make when using a chicken or chickens for another dish or preparing several chickens for the deep freeze. (Serves 4–6, hot)

2 sets chicken giblets
1 large onion
2–3 carrots
2–3 stalks celery
chicken skin and carcass (if available)
5 cups water
4–5 parsley stalks, 1 sprig of thyme, 1 bay leaf tied together
6 peppercorns
chicken cube (optional)
2 tablespoons butter
1½ tablespoons flour

GARNISH
1 tablespoon butter
2 chicken livers
2 tablespoons chopped parsley

1. Wash the chicken giblets, removing the livers. Reserve these for garnish.
2. Peel and slice the onion, carrots and celery. Put these into a pan with the giblets—and any skin or carcass from the chicken. Add the water, herbs, peppercorns and some salt. Bring slowly to a boil, skimming off any scum that rises to the top. Reduce heat, and simmer for 1–1½ hours until the vegetables are tender and the giblets well cooked. Taste soup: if not well flavored a chicken cube can be added. (Remove skin and carcass, or strain soup into another pan.)
3. Melt the butter and blend in the flour. Strain on to the chicken stock, blend thoroughly and bring to a boil, stirring constantly. Cook for a few minutes.
4. Cook the chicken livers gently in 1 tablespoon butter for about 5–8 minutes depending on their size. Chop livers roughly and divide between soup cups before pouring on hot soup. Sprinkle with chopped parsley.

Turkey and Chestnut Soup

carcass of one cooked turkey
3–4 tablespoons or more of leftover chestnut stuffing (or 5–6 tablespoons canned chestnut purée)
2 onions, sliced
2–3 carrots, sliced
2–3 stalks of celery, sliced
several sprigs of parsley
1 bay leaf
5–6 cups water
1 tablespoon butter
¾ tablespoon all purpose flour

GARNISH
5–6 chestnuts
1 tablespoon chopped parsley

A delicious soup made from the remains of the Thanksgiving or Christmas Day turkey and chestnut stuffing (Serves 4–6, hot)

1. Remove the remaining chestnut stuffing from the cold turkey and reserve. Take off any pieces of turkey meat which can be used as a garnish. Break up the turkey carcass and put into a large pan with sliced onions, carrots, celery and herbs. Cover with water and simmer until well flavored. Avoid boiling hard as this makes stock cloudy. Strain.

2. Put the chestnut stuffing into the electric blender with a cup of turkey stock and blend until smooth. Turn into a pan and add the remaining 4 cups stock, seasoning and the turkey meat. Cook together for a few minutes. If the soup is too thin, blend the butter and flour together to make a paste, add to the soup in small pieces, and stir until thickened.
3. Bring to a boil, and serve hot with a few cooked chestnuts, fried in butter and broken into pieces, and sprinkled on top with chopped parsley.

Chinese Chicken Soup

- 4–5 spring onions
- 6 small mushrooms, finely sliced
- 5 cups of strongly-flavored clear chicken stock
- 2 cups shredded white chicken meat
- 2 beaten eggs
- 2–3 teaspoons soy sauce

Light chicken soup with mushrooms, spring onions, beaten egg and chicken shreds cooked in boiling soup (Serves 4–6, hot)

1. Finely slice the white part of the spring onions and reserve the green part for garnish. Heat the chicken stock until boiling. Add the mushrooms and onions, and cook for 2–3 minutes. Add the shredded white chicken meat.

2. Beat the eggs until frothy with a little salt and pepper.

3. Stir the soup well. Then pour the beaten egg steadily into the soup, stirring constantly, so that it remains in shreds. Allow to cook for a minute or two to set egg. Add soy sauce to taste and serve in soup bowls, sprinkled with the finely chopped green parts of the spring onions.

Mock Bouillabaise *(see p. 33)*

Game Soup

5 cups of well-flavored game stock (made from carcass and meat of any game available)
1 onion, diced
2 small carrots, diced
2 stalks celery, sliced
1 bay leaf, 1 sprig of thyme, 3–4 sprigs of parsley, tied together
1 tablespoon redcurrant or other sharp jelly
1 small glass port (or sherry)
½ cup diced cooked game (if available)
a dash of lemon juice

GARNISH
1 tablespoon chopped parsley
fried bread croutons (see garnish section)

Game stock with cooked vegetables and additions of sherry and sharp jelly (Serves 4–6, hot)

1. Put strained stock into a soup pot, having first skimmed off the fat. Add the herbs and diced raw vegetables, and cook these in the simmering stock until they are tender. Avoid boiling the soup as this makes the stock cloudy. Add the redcurrant or other sharp jelly, and let dissolve. Remove herbs and add port (or sherry) and the diced cooked game if available. Heat through. Season to taste, and add a dash of lemon juice.
2. Sprinkle with chopped parsley, and serve with fried bread croutons.

Pheasant Soup

A clear soup made with pheasant carcass, garnished with pheasant meat, mushrooms and vegetables (Serves 4–6, hot)

1 pheasant carcass
5–6 cups water
1 onion, sliced
2 carrots, sliced
2 stalks celery, sliced
4 sprigs of parsley
1 small bay leaf
3–4 peppercorns
4–6 mushrooms, finely sliced
½ cup cooked peas
½ cup diced cooked pheasant meat
1 small glass sherry (or port)
2 tablespoons chopped parsley

1. Break the carcass into pieces and put into pan with the water, onion, carrots and celery. Add the herbs and some seasoning. Bring to a boil, and simmer for 30 minutes to 1 hour, until it is well flavored. Strain through a fine sieve.

2. Add the mushrooms to the soup and cook for a few minutes. Add the peas and pheasant meat and heat through. Just before serving, add the sherry (or port) and serve hot, sprinkled with chopped parsley.

Chicken and Ham Soup

Clear chicken soup, with a garnish of finely shredded lean ham and cooked peas (Serves 4–6, hot or cold)

4–5 cups of clear chicken stock (or consomme)
1 glass white wine
2 slices of mild ham
½ cup lightly cooked fresh peas
1 teaspoon chopped (or ½ teaspoon dried) tarragon
1 tablespoon chopped parsley
1–1½ tablespoons gelatine for cold soup

1. If serving hot, heat the clear chicken stock, adding at the last minute a glass of white wine, the shredded ham which has had all the fat removed, the lightly cooked green peas and herbs. Serve hot. Sprinkle with chopped parsley.

2. If serving cold and using chicken stock which is not already jellied, put gelatine to soak in ½ cup of stock. When it has swollen, heat gently and add to the heated stock. Skim off any grease carefully, add the white wine and let cool in a bowl. When it is on the point of setting, add the shreds of ham and the peas, and spoon into soup cups. Chill well and serve garnished with chopped parsley or watercress leaves.

White Fish Chowder, *see right*

6 FISH SOUPS

Clam Chowder

A traditional American chowder which is a delicious meal in itself (Serves 4, hot)

3–4 quarts clams in shells, preferably hard backs (or 1½–2 cups chopped canned clams)
2 cups water
1–1½ inch cube of fat salt pork (or 2 slices of fat bacon)
1 onion, finely sliced
1 cup diced potato
1 bay leaf
1 tablespoon parsley
¼ teaspoon thyme
1–1½ cups chicken stock if using canned clams; reduce to ¾ cup if using raw clams
2 cups canned tomatoes
½ green pepper, seeded and diced
2 tablespoons butter
paprika

1. If using fresh clams, scrub the shells well and wash carefully in several changes of cold water. Put into a soup pot and pour over 2 cups water. Cover the pot tightly and bring to a boil slowly. When boiling point is reached remove from heat and leave for a minute. Strain through muslin (to catch any sand) and reserve juice. Cool clams, remove from shells, and chop. If using canned clams, merely chop, drain and reserve liquid.

2. Chop the fat salt pork or fat bacon, and heat gently until fat melts and the bacon is crisp. Remove any crisp pieces of pork or bacon and reserve.

3. Cook the onion gently in fat for 4–5 minutes without browning. Add the potato, bay leaf, parsley and thyme. Pour on the stock, heat gently to boiling point and cook for 10 minutes, adding seasoning to taste. Add the tomatoes and green peppers. Cook for 5–7 minutes.

4. Add the chopped clams and their liquid, and cook for long enough to heat through thoroughly without boiling. Add crispy pieces of bacon. Just before serving, stir in the butter. Place in soup plates and sprinkle with paprika.

5. Serve with plain crackers, which can be crumbled into the chowder if desired.

White Fish Chowder

A substantial thick soup of fish and potatoes, which can make a meal in itself (Serves 4–6, hot)

1 pound fresh cod, haddock or halibut, fileted
head, skin and bones of fish
2 cups water
2 onions, 1 sliced, 1 chopped
1 carrot, sliced
1 bay leaf
3–4 sprigs of parsley (or 1 tablespoon dried parsley)
1 small cube of fat salt port (about 1 inch) or 2–3 slices of fat bacon
1 cup diced potatoes
2 cups milk
¼ teaspoon ground mace or nutmeg
1 tablespoon chopped fennel
1 tablespoon chopped parsley
2 tablespoons butter

1. Wash the fish skin, head and bones in cold water, and put into a pan with 2 cups of water. Add 1 onion, carrot, bay leaf, parsley sprigs, salt and pepper. Bring slowly to a boil, skimming as necessary. Reduce heat, and simmer for 15–20 minutes. Strain, and reserve liquid for chowder.

2. Chop the fat salt pork or bacon, and cook slowly until the fat melts. Remove the crispy pieces of bacon, and reserve for garnish.

3. Chop the second onion and add to the hot fat. Cook gently until tender. Then add the diced potatoes and the fish stock. Cook for 5–6 minutes before adding the fish chunks. Then simmer until the potatoes are tender and the fish cooked, about 10 minutes.

4. Bring the milk to nearly boiling point and add to the fish mixture with seasoning and herbs. When ready to serve, stir in the butter, and serve at once.

Shrimp Bisque

A rich party soup with flavor of shrimp, heightened by the addition of sherry or brandy (Serves 4–6, hot–see picture, p. 4)

2 pounds shrimp
3 cups chicken stock
3 tablespoons butter
1 onion, sliced
1 carrot, sliced
1 stalk celery, sliced
3 tablespoons rice
1 bay leaf
3–4 sprigs of parsley (or 1 tablespoon dried parsley)
a squeeze of lemon juice
¼ teaspoon ground mace
1 cup heavy cream
3 tablespoons brandy or sherry

1. Remove the shells from the shrimp, and wash in cold water. Reserve ½ cup shrimp for garnish. Put the shells into a pan with the stock, and simmer gently for 20 minutes.

2. Melt the butter, and cook the onion, carrot and celery for 4–5 minutes to soften. Add the rice, the shrimp, roughly chopped, the herbs, lemon juice and seasoning. Cook together for a minute. Then strain over the stock. Bring to a boil, and simmer for 20 minutes.

3. Remove the bay leaf. Put the soup into electric blender and blend until smooth or put through a fine food mill or sieve.

4. Return soup to pan, add the reserved ½ cup of shrimp. Re-heat and adjust seasoning. Add the heated cream, and just before serving, add the brandy or sherry.

Moules Marinière

A succulent mussel soup, eaten from deep soup plates. It is extremely filling and can be used as a main course (Serves 4, hot)

40–50 mussels fresh and unopened
1 onion or 4–5 shallots
1 carrot
1 stalk celery
1 clove garlic
1 cup white wine
1 cup water
2 tablespoons chopped parsley
1 bay leaf
a pinch of thyme
3 tablespoons butter
2½ tablespoons flour

1. Wash the mussels and scrub thoroughly to remove weed or sand. Knock or scrape off barnacles. Remove the beards. Examine mussels carefully, and if any are not tightly closed discard immediately, as they are poisonous if not alive when cooked. Soak the mussels in plenty of cold water, as they will expel any sand from inside the shells during soaking process.

2. Meanwhile, chop the onion or shallots, peel and chop the carrot and slice celery. Crush the garlic and add to the pan with wine, water, 1 tablespoon of chopped parsley, the bay leaf, thyme and ground black pepper. Bring to a boil, and then simmer for 6–8 minutes.

3. Drain the mussels and add to the pan. Cover tightly with a lid and simmer for 6–8 minutes, shaking the pan frequently to make sure that all mussels are covered by liquid. Remove from heat as soon as the mussels open their shells.

4. Strain off liquid and reserve. Remove mussels from pan and carefully remove half of each shell. If serving for a party carefully remove the inner part of gristly beard; otherwise, each diner can do this for himself at the table. Put the half shells holding the fish into a deep dish and keep warm.

5. Put cooking liquid into a pan. Blend the butter and flour into a paste, and add to the liquid. Bring slowly to a boil, whisking constantly. Add the second tablespoonful of chopped parsley. Adjust seasoning, and pour over the mussels.

6. Serve in deep soup plates.

Lobster Bisque

A party soup with a rich and never-to-be-forgotten flavor (Serves 6, hot)

- 1 large freshly boiled lobster (or 2 small, preferably female, lobsters)
- 5–6 cups fish stock
- 1 small onion, sliced
- 1 carrot, sliced
- 2 stalks celery, sliced
- 1 bay leaf, 3–4 sprigs of parsley, tied together
- 5 tablespoons butter
- 2½ tablespoons flour
- ¼ teaspoon mace or nutmeg
- 1 cup cream
- 3–4 tablespoons sherry (or brandy)

1. Split the freshly boiled lobster down the back with a sharp knife and remove the intestine, which looks like a long black thread down the center of the back. Also remove the stomach sac from head and the tough gills. Crack the claws, remove the meat and add this to the back meat. If the lobster is female and there is red coral or roe: reserve this for garnish. Also reserve the greenish curd from the head.

2. Break up all the lobster shells and put into a pan with the fish stock. Add the onion, carrot, celery, herbs, salt and pepper. Cover the pan and simmer for 30–45 minutes.

3. Meanwhile, cut the lobster meat into chunks. Pound the coral roe with 2 tablespoons butter to use as garnish and to color soup.

4. Melt 3 tablespoons butter in a pot, stir in the flour until smoothly blended, cook for a minute or two before adding the strained lobster stock. Blend until smooth and then bring to a boil, stirring constantly. Reduce heat, and simmer for 4–5 minutes before adding the lobster meat. Remove herbs. Add the mace or nutmeg, and adjust seasoning. Lastly, add the cup of hot cream and the sherry (or brandy).

5. Serve in soup cups with a piece of the coral butter in each cup and sprinkle with paprika.

Mock Bouillabaisse

True bouillabaisse, a rich fish soup originating from the Mediterranean area, requires special fish not readily available, but a delicious imitation can be made. This is a very filling soup, and it is fairly complicated to make it is only worth preparing for a large number of people (Serves 6–8, hot–see picture, p. 29)

- ½ cup olive oil
- 2 medium onions, chopped
- 2 leeks, chopped
- 2 carrots, chopped
- 1–2 cloves of garlic, crushed
- 2 lbs mixed fish: red snapper, flounder, whiting, halibut, perch, red mullet, haddock, eel
- 4 ripe tomatoes (or ½ cup canned tomatoes)
- 1 bay leaf
- 1 tablespoon chopped fennel
- a pinch of saffron soaked in boiling water
- 1 sprig of thyme
- 4–5 parsley stalks chopped
- 2–3 thinly peeled pieces of orange zest
- 2–3 cups fish stock or water
- ¾–1 cup shrimp, clams, and lobster meat
- 1 teaspoon lemon juice
- 1 cup white wine
- 6–8 slices of French bread

GARNISH
- 2 tablespoons butter
- 1 clove garlic, crushed
- 2 tablespoons chopped parsley

1. Heat the oil in a large pan. Add the onions, leeks, carrots and garlic. Cook slowly until golden brown, stirring frequently to prevent burning.

2. Add the fish, which should be boneless and cut into chunks. Add the peeled, chopped tomatoes (or canned tomatoes), bay leaf, fennel, saffron, thyme, parsley, orange zest, fish stock or water, salt and pepper. Cover the pan, and cook for 15–20 minutes.

3. Then add the shellfish, leaving the shrimp whole but cutting the clam or lobster meat into chunks (canned minced clams and canned lobster meat can be used). Bring to a boil, and cook for 6–8 minutes. Then add lemon juice and wine. Re-heat for a few more minutes, and adjust seasoning.

4. While the soup is cooking, cut the French bread into ½-inch slices and put into a warm oven to bake hard. Mix the softened butter with a crushed clove of garlic, add pepper and salt. Spread this paste on to the bread slices.

5. Put a slice of bread into the bottom of each soup cup or plate. Carefully spoon the pieces of fish and shellfish into the soup cups, dividing equally; then spoon over the broth, sprinkle with chopped parsley and serve at once.

Pink Fish Soup

1 pound fileted white fish
STOCK
skin, bones and heads of several fish
5 cups water
2 onions
1 carrot
several sprigs of parsley (or 1 tablespoon chopped parsley)
1 bay leaf
1 sprig (or ¼ teaspoon chopped) thyme
6 peppercorns
½ teaspoon salt

SOUP
3 tablespoons butter
1 onion, finely chopped
2 small carrots, finely sliced
2 leeks, sliced
1 stalk celery, sliced
1 clove garlic, crushed
2 tablespoons flour
2 tablespoons tomato purée
1 cup canned tomatoes sieved
sugar and mace or nutmeg to taste
1 tablespoon chopped parsley and fennel
½ cup peeled fresh (or canned) shrimp or flaked cooked (or canned) salmon

GARNISH
paprika
garlic croutons (see garnish section)

A very filling and attractively colored fish soup, which can be used as a main course for a family lunch (Serves 6, hot)

1. Skin and filet fish if not already prepared. Cut the fish into bite sized chunks, and put in refrigerator while making stock.

2. Wash the skin head and bones of fish and put in pan with 5 cups water, peeled and quartered onions, and carrot, herbs, peppercorns and salt. Bring to a boil. Then lower heat, and simmer gently for 20–30 minutes. Then strain and reserve stock for soup.

3. Melt butter. Add the onion, carrots, leeks, celery and garlic, and cook gently for 5–6 minutes with lid on pan, until they are tender. Sprinkle in the flour and blend well. Add the tomato purée and tomatoes, stirring until well mixed. Add seasoning and herbs, cover pan and cook gently for 10–15 minutes. Pour in the fish stock, add the fish chunks, bring the soup to a boil and simmer for 10 minutes.

4. Add the shrimp, or flaked cooked salmon or canned salmon. Heat through and adjust seasoning. Sprinkle with paprika, and serve with garlic croutons.

Maryland Crab Soup

6 cups strong beef stock
3 cups mixed vegetables (fresh, left-over or frozen—include chopped onions and celery, diced carrots, peas, lima beans, cut string beans, corn, okra and tomatoes, not squash, cabbage or potatoes)
1 pound crab meat (claw or white meat)
seafood seasoning to taste
claws and pieces of whole crab if available (either raw or cooked)

A hearty, highly flavored seafood favorite (Serves 4–6, hot)

1. Heat the stock in a large soup pot. Add the vegetables and seasoning, and simmer for 1 hour.

2. Add the crab meat and the crab claws and pieces (if available) 30 minutes before serving. Simmer gently, to heat through and allow flavors to blend.

3. Serve hot in large soup bowls, with bread and butter or hard crusty rolls and butter as accompaniment.

7 CONSOMMES

Consomme Madrilene

Clear tomato-flavored chicken consomme (Serves 4–6, hot or cold)

1 pound ripe tomatoes
5 cups well-flavored, clear jellied chicken stock
1 cup chopped lean beef
¼ cup sherry (or white wine)
1 tablespoon parsley
1 teaspoon basil
a pinch of sugar
2 egg whites and shells of two eggs

GARNISH
1 large tomato peeled and cut into strips, if hot
lemon quarters and cheese straws (see garnish section) if cold

1. Chop the tomatoes and put into an enamel or heat-proof glass pan. Add well-flavored jellied chicken stock, which has been skimmed to remove fat. Add chopped lean raw beef, sherry or white wine, herbs, sugar and seasoning.

2. Beat the egg whites until frothy but not stiff. Add to the soup pan with the finely crushed egg shells. Bring the soup very slowly to a boil, whisking thoroughly the whole time. When soup is just reaching boiling point and is rising up in the pan stop whisking, remove pan from heat to allow the egg white crust to subside, then leave pan on a very low heat for 30–40 minutes.

3. Put a piece of clean cloth over a fine sieve and strain soup carefully, allowing the egg white crust to slide on to the cloth. Pour soup through this filter again, by which time it should be clear. Adjust seasoning.

4. Prepare garnish: Dip 1 large tomato into boiling water for the count of ten and then in cold water. Remove skin and seeds, and cut the tomato flesh into strips. Add to soup just before serving. If serving cold, let cool, and set in refrigerator. Then stir with a fork. Serve in chilled soup cups with lemon quarters and cheese straws.

Tomato Consomme Madras

A most unusual cold soup of consomme, flavored with curry and tomato and garnished with lemon mayonnaise and chives (Serves 4–6, cold)

2 cans of jellied condensed consomme
1 small bottle of tomato juice cocktail, with tabasco or Worcestershire sauce added
2 teaspoons curry powder (or paste)
a few drops lemon juice
3 tablespoons fresh mayonnaise
grated lemon rind to taste
1–2 teaspoons lemon juice
1 tablespoon heavy cream, whipped
2 teaspoons chopped chives

1. Heat the consomme very slightly to dissolve it. Add the tomato juice and the curry powder (or paste). Mix in thoroughly. Add a little lemon juice.

2. Pour into the soup cups and let chill.

3. Mix the mayonnaise with grated lemon rind and juice. Add the whipped cream. Put a spoonful of this mayonnaise on to the center of each cup of jellied soup and sprinkle with chopped chives. Serve with brown bread and butter.

Consomme a La Princesse

Clear consomme garnished with diced cooked chicken and asparagus tips (Serves 4–6, hot)

2–3 tablespoons asparagus tips
1 small cooked chicken breast
4–5 cups clear chicken or beef consomme
a little sherry (optional)
1 tablespoon finely chopped parsley

1. Cook the asparagus tips, if fresh, in boiling water; if canned, rinse and heat in a little of the liquid from the can. Dice the white chicken meat.

2. Heat the clear chicken or beef consomme. Add a little sherry if desired, the asparagus tips and the chicken dice, and heat through.

3. Serve hot with the asparagus and chicken divided between soup cups. Sprinkle with finely chopped parsley.

Clear Beet Consomme

Clear ruby red consomme with highly individual flavor heightened by garnish of sour cream (Serves 4–6, hot or cold)

4–5 cups clear jellied brown or chicken stock
2–3 small well-colored cooked red beets
1–2 teaspoons onion juice
juice of approx half a lemon

GARNISH
4–6 tablespoons sour cream
piroshki (see garnish section)
1 lemon cut in quarters or sixths

1. First prepare clear jellied stock. Either chicken or brown stock may be used, or use canned jellied consomme to make equivalent quantity. Put 4–5 cups of stock or consomme into pan with the grated peeled beets, the onion juice (made by squeezing small pieces of cut onion in a garlic press) and some seasoning if necessary, although the stock should be well flavored.

2. Bring the soup slowly to a moderate heat and let it cook very gently for 30–40 minutes or until the soup is well flavored and colored by the beets. Do not let it boil as this makes the soup a muddy brown color instead of a rich red.

3. Strain soup through a double layer of clean cloth. Add enough lemon juice to sharpen the flavor and adjust seasoning. If serving hot, re-heat to just below boiling point and serve with a garnish of sour cream, handed separately, and with piroshki. If serving cold, put into a clean bowl and chill in refrigerator. Mix with a fork before serving with lemon quarters and sour cream.

Poor Millionaire's Consomme I

Delectable combination of sherry-flavored consomme, topped with black or red caviar and cream (Serves 4–6, cold)

2 cans of condensed consomme (or 3–4 cups well-flavored home-made consomme
1–2 tablespoons sherry
a squeeze of lemon juice
1 small jar of caviar (black or red)
1 small carton of sour cream or fresh thick cream made sour with lemon juice
a pinch of onion or garlic powder (optional)
paprika or 1–2 teaspoons chopped chives

GARNISH
cheese straws (see garnish section)
lemon quarters

1. Heat the jellied or canned consomme very slightly until it just dissolves. Add the sherry and a few drops of lemon juice to sharpen flavor. Pour into the soup cups allowing space at the top for the garnish, then chill until thoroughly set.

2. Place a large teaspoon of caviar in a mound on top of each cup of jellied soup.

3. Mix salt, pepper, onion or garlic powder (if desired) and paprika into the sour cream, and spoon this mixture over the caviar.

4. Sprinkle the top with paprika or chopped chives, and serve with cheese straws and lemon quarters.

Consomme Julienne

Clear soup with a garnish of strips of cooked vegetables (Serves 4–6, hot)

4–5 cups clear beef consomme
2 small carrots
2–3 sticks celery, white part only
1 leek, white part only
1 cup stock
2–3 tablespoons sherry

1. Prepare the vegetables by cutting into even, match-like strips. Put into a pan, and cover with a little stock and seasoning. Cook gently until just tender. Drain, reserving the stock for use in another soup or sauce.

2. Heat the clear consomme and add a little sherry. Add the julienne of vegetables, and serve hot.

Beef Consomme

Clear, strongly flavored beef soup which can be served hot or cold and jellied

1 pound of lean beef
10 cups rich beef stock made from raw bones and meat
2 egg whites
egg shells of two eggs.
4–5 tablespoons sherry

1. Cut the lean beef into small pieces and put into pan with the rich brown stock, which had been specially made with bones, vegetables, herbs and seasonings.

2. Beat the egg whites until frothy but not stiff. Wash the egg shells, crumple them into the whites and add all this mixture to the soup pan. Heat the soup gently while whisking the egg white mixture into it with a wire whisk using a backward beating movement. When just reaching boiling point remove whisk and allow soup to rise in the pan. Then remove quickly from heat, and when it subsides again continue to cook on a very low heat for 35–45 minutes to allow meat juices and flavor to blend into soup.

3. Put a piece of cheese cloth or a clean cloth over a fine sieve and strain the soup through this, allowing the egg-white crust to slide on to the cloth. Pour the soup back through this filter and if necessary repeat a second time to make soup completely clear. Add sherry and seasoning if necessary, and serve hot or chilled.

Poor Millionaire's Consomme II

Tomato-flavored chicken consomme, chilled and garnished with fresh shrimp (Serves 4–6, cold)

2 cans of chicken consomme (or 3–4 cups clear chicken jellied stock)
3–4 ripe red tomatoes, peeled, seeded and chopped
2 thin strips of finely pared lemon rind
a little red vegetable coloring (if needed)
1 teaspoon lemon juice
24–36 peeled freshly boiled shrimp
4–6 thin slices lemon

1. Heat the jellied chicken stock or canned consomme gently with the peeled, seeded, chopped tomatoes, seasoning (if necessary) and lemon rind. Simmer for 20–30 minutes or until the soup is well flavored and colored. Strain and cool.

2. If the soup is not a clear red add a little food coloring. Add lemon juice and adjust seasoning.

3. Chill in a bowl in refrigerator. When set break up slightly with a fork and spoon into soup cups.

4. Garnish with freshly cooked shrimp. Canned or frozen shellfish can be used but may need to be soaked in a little French dressing to improve the flavor. Decorate with lemon curls.

Consomme Royale

Clear consomme served with a garnish of Royale custard (Serves 4–6, hot)

4–5 cups clear beef consommé or canned consommé
2–3 tablespoons sherry

ROYALE GARNISH
1 whole egg
2 egg yolks
½ cup cream
4–5 tablespoons consommé
a pinch of mace
¼ teaspoon chopped chervil

1. First make Royale garnish. Beat the whole egg and the egg yolks well together. Mix the cream with 4–5 tablespoons consomme. Add a good pinch of salt, pepper, mace and the chervil if available. Add the eggs to this creamy mixture, and mix well together. Butter the sides of a baking pan or a fire-proof dish or bowl and pour in the custard. Cover tightly with foil, and stand it in a pan of hot water which should reach half way up the sides of the baking pan or dish. Cook in a slow oven (300°F) until the custard is set, 15–20 minutes or more. Let cool. Turn out cold custard and cut into slices. Cut slices into small shapes—diamonds, crescents, stars etc.—and use as garnish for soup.

2. Heat the clear consomme, add seasoning to taste and sherry. Pour into soup cups. Add the Royale garnish and serve hot.

Creamy Consomme Philadelphia

A wonderful light creamy mixture of consomme and cream cheese (Serves 4–6, cold)

2 cans condensed consomme
2 small or one medium package of cream cheese (Philadelphia if available)
a few drops tabasco
a few drops onion juice (or garlic juice, or powder)
1–2 tablespoons cream
1–2 tablespoons sherry

GARNISH
2–3 teaspoons chopped chives or a sprinkling of paprika
hot garlic bread (see garnish section)

1. Reserve just over a quarter of one can of consomme for garnish. Put remainder into electric blender with the cream cheese, tabasco, onion or crushed garlic, salt and pepper to taste. Blend gently until smooth, adding a little cream if necessary.

2. Taste and adjust seasoning. Pour into soup cups and chill, covered with paper or foil to prevent garlic odor getting into refrigerator.

3. Heat the remaining consomme until just melted but not hot. Add sherry. Let cool and when the soup is set, spoon a thin layer of this garnishing mixture on to each cup and chill again. When set sprinkle with chopped chives or a little paprika.

4. Serve cold with hot garlic bread.

Variation

Creamy Shrimp Consomme

Shrimp-flavored creamy consomme chilled soup (Serves 4–6, cold)

3–5 tablespoons shrimp

1. Use same ingredients as above adding 2–3 tablespoons shrimp to blender, and using two full cans of consomme.

2. The garnish in this case is 3–4 whole shrimp to each cup and a sprinkling of chopped parsley or paprika.

Variation

Creamy Curry Consomme

Curry-flavored creamy consomme (Serves 4–6, cold)

1½–teaspoons curry powder (or paste)
a squeeze of lemon juice
lemon slices

1. Use same ingredients and method as first recipe, but add 1½–2 teaspoons curry powder or paste to the blender and also a squeeze of lemon juice.

2. Garnish with very thin slices of lemon.

Variation

Creamy Tomato Consomme

Tomato-flavored creamy consomme (Serves 4–6, cold)

1½–2 tablespoons tomato purée
a squeeze of lemon juice
1–2 tomatoes, sliced (or shredded)
2–3 teaspoons chopped parsley (or chives)

1. Use same ingredients and method as first recipe, but add 1½–2 tablespoons tomato purée to mixture in blender and also a squeeze of lemon juice.

2. Garnish with slices of peeled, sliced tomato or thin strips of tomato flesh, with seeds removed, and a little chopped parsley or chives.

8 SOUPS WITH A DIFFERENCE

Eastern Avocado Soup

2–3 avocados, rather over-ripe
4 cups tomato juice
3–4 teaspoons curry powder (or paste)
2–3 teaspoons lemon juice
1 cup chicken stock
1 small carton yogurt
1 cup cream

GARNISH
1 tablespoon chopped chives (or 1 tablespoon chopped nuts)
lemon quarters
brown bread and butter or crackers

A lightly curried and tomato-flavored avocado soup: a useful way to use rather over-ripe avocados (Serves 6, cold)

1. Peel and remove seeds from avocados. Put in an electric blender, adding a can of tomato juice, 3–4 teaspoons of curry powder, according to taste, and stock. When blended, add lemon juice, yogurt, and salt and pepper to taste. Blend again.

2. Chill in refrigerator until just before serving, when the lightly whipped cream should be stirred into the soup, leaving a streaky appearance.

3. Sprinkle with chopped chives or chopped nuts, and serve with lemon quarters and brown bread and butter or crackers.

Danish Apple Soup

1½ lbs cooking apples
5 cups water
6–8 strips of thinly pared lemon rind
juice of half a lemon
½ cup granulated sugar
1–1½ tablespoons cornstarch
½ cup heavy cream

GARNISH
grated lemon rind, if hot
thin slices of lemon, if cold

Lemon-flavored apple soup—delicious served chilled on a hot summer night, but also good hot (Serves 4–6, hot or cold)

1. Wash and quarter apples removing cores and peel. Put into a pan with water and thinly pared lemon rind. Cook with lid on pan until the apples are soft, about 20–25 minutes.

2. Strain the liquid from the pan. Put apple pulp through a fine sieve or food mill, or blend until smooth in an electric blender, adding the liquid gradually and mixing well with the sugar and lemon juice.

3. Mix the cornstarch with a little cold water. Add a few spoonfuls of hot soup, and mix well before adding to the soup. Bring soup to a boil, and cook for 4–5 minutes to cook cornstarch.

4. Stir in cream just before serving, and sprinkle top of each soup cup with finely grated lemon rind. If serving cold, add the cream when the soup is cold and serve with a thin slice of lemon on top of each soup cup.

Danish Mushroom Soup

2–3 tablespoons butter
1 onion, finely sliced
2 cups sliced white mushrooms
2 tablespoons flour
4 cups clear beef stock or 2 cans consomme
1 tablespoon chopped parsley
1 teaspoon chopped tarragon
½ cup cream
4 tablespoons sherry

Party soup with a deliciously different flavor (Serves 4–6, hot)

1. Melt the butter, and cook the onion gently with lid on pan for 3–5 minutes, without browning. Add mushrooms, and cook for a minute or two more. Sprinkle in the flour. When blended, add the stock or canned consomme. Bring slowly to a boil, stirring constantly, and simmer for 10–15 minutes. Add seasoning.

2. Just before serving add herbs, cream and sherry. Serve at once.

Iced Avocado Soup

Creamy luxurious soup for a summer dinner party (Serves 6, cold)

2–3 ripe avocados
4 teaspoons lemon juice
1 teaspoon onion juice
a dash of tabasco
3 cups chicken stock
1 small carton yogurt (natural)
¼ teaspoon nutmeg
¾ cup heavy cream
1–2 teaspoons chopped fresh dill or a few fresh tarragon leaves

GARNISH
cheese straws (see garnish section)
or rolls of brown bread and butter sprinkled with chopped walnuts

1. Peel avocados. Reserve a quarter of one avocado to use as garnish; sprinkle it with lemon juice and cover it with a plastic wrap to prevent browning. Mash the remaining avocado with 2–3 teaspoons lemon juice. Make onion juice by crushing small pieces of onion in a garlic press or squeezing through a fine sieve. Add this juice and a dash of tabasco to the avocado.

2. Put all these ingredients into electric blender and add the chicken stock by degrees, blending slowly. When smooth add the natural yogurt. Blend again, and when thoroughly mixed add salt, pepper and nutmeg to taste.

3. Add half the cream to the soup, stirring it in only partially to give a marbled appearance to soup. Pour into soup cups and chill.

4. Just before serving beat remaining cream and cut the ¼ of avocado into thin slivers. Slide these into soup cups. Put a spoonful of whipped cream into each cup and sprinkle top with chopped fresh dill or a few tarragon leaves.

5. Serve with hot cheese straws or rolls or brown bread and butter sprinkled with chopped walnuts.

Danish Beer Soup

A very unusual soup, suitable for breakfast on cold mornings (Serves 4, hot)

6–7 slices rye or pumpernickel bread
2 cups water
2 cups brown ale or beer
grated rind and juice of 1 small lemon
sugar to taste

GARNISH
whipped cream, or milk

1. Crumble the rye or pumpernickel bread and soak in water overnight or for at least 3–4 hours. Add the ale or beer and bring to a boil, stirring constantly. Then simmer until the bread disintegrates into a thickish brown soup.

2. Blend in electric blender with lemon rind and juice, and sugar to taste. Re-heat, and serve with whipped cream on top, or milk to thin slightly.

Vichyssoise

A creamy and delicately flavored cold party soup, made with leeks and potatoes (Serves 4–6, cold)

3 medium leeks
4 tablespoons butter
1 medium onion, finely sliced
3 medium potatoes, finely sliced
4 cups chicken stock
¼ teaspoon mace
1 bay leaf
1–2 cups cream

GARNISH
1 tablespoon chopped chives
brown bread and butter, or crisp melba toast

1. Wash the white part of leeks carefully, slice finely and wash again to remove any clinging sand or earth. Melt the butter and add the leeks, onion and potatoes. Turn in the butter over a low heat until all are coated in butter. Cover the pan and cook very gently without allowing to brown, as this will ruin color and flavor of soup. Stir and shake pan from time to time until the vegetables are soft. Pour on the chicken stock and add salt, pepper, mace and bay leaf. Simmer gently for 20 minutes.

2. Remove bay leaf. Pour soup into electric blender and blend until smooth, or put through fine food mill. Then pour through sieve into a bowl to cool.

3. Add the cream and adjust seasoning, then chill.

4. Sprinkle with chopped chives, and serve with brown bread and butter or crisp melba toast.

Hot Avocado and Prawn Soup

Unusual and quickly made party soup (Serves 4–6, hot)

1 small onion, finely chopped
2 stalks celery, finely chopped
3–4 cups well-flavored chicken stock
1 small bay leaf
a blade or pinch of mace
3–4 sprigs of parsley
2–3 avocados (according to size)
½ cup peeled shrimp

GARNISH
1 cup heavy cream
chopped chives or paprika
slivers of fresh avocado

1. Put the onion and celery into the stock with the bay leaf, mace, sprigs of parsley and a little seasoning. Simmer for about 15 minutes to flavor stock. Strain and reserve stock.

2. Peel and remove seeds from avocados, and chop the flesh roughly. Put into electric blender, and blend slowly while adding the stock. When quite smooth, return to pan and heat very gently, adding the shrimp. Do not allow to boil, as this will spoil flavor and texture of soup. Adjust seasoning.

3. Whip the cream slightly and add a spoon of cream to each soup cup. Sprinkle top with paprika or chopped chives, and add a few thin slivers of another avocado as party garnish.

Creamy Cucumber Soup

Delicately flavored cucumber soup, suitable for a dinner party (Serves 4–6, hot)

2–3 medium cucumbers
4–5 spring onions (or 3 shallots) chopped finely
3 tablespoons butter
2 tablespoons flour
4 cups chicken stock or white stock (or water and cubes)
¼ teaspoon mace
a pinch of sugar
1 tablespoon chopped parsley
1 teaspoon chopped dill
a little green coloring (if necessary)
2 egg yolks
½ cup heavy cream

GARNISH
2 teaspoons chopped dill
fried bread croutons (see garnish section)

1. Peel and quarter the cucumbers, remove and discard seeds. Cut into small dice. Reserve 4–5 tablespoons of cucumber dice to use as garnish: sprinkle these with salt, and let stand for 20 minutes before washing and draining. Melt the butter and cook the onions (or shallots) very gently for 5 minutes to soften without browning. Add the larger amount of cucumber dice and cook gently for 2–3 minutes, stirring frequently.

2. Sprinkle in flour, blend smoothly before adding stock. Bring to a boil, stirring constantly. Add herbs and seasonings, then simmer gently for 15 minutes or until vegetables are tender.

3. Put soup into electric blender and blend until smooth, or put through food mill. Return to pot and re-heat. Add a little green coloring and adjust seasoning to taste.

4. Make liaison: mix the egg yolks and cream well, add a few spoonfuls of hot soup, and mix well before straining into soup, whisking constantly. Heat soup gently, but do not boil, as this causes the egg yolk to curdle.

5. Just before serving add the raw, drained cucumber dice, and sprinkle each soup cup with a little chopped dill. Serve with fried bread croutons.

Avgolemno Soup

Traditional Greek light lemon-flavored soup (Serves 4–6, hot or cold)

5 cups strong chicken stock
2–3 tablespoons rice
2 eggs or 3 egg yolks
1 large or 2 small lemons
4–6 tablespoons heavy cream
chopped parsley

1. Heat the strongly-flavored chicken stock in a pan. When boiling, add rice and cook for 12 minutes or until rice is cooked.

2. Meanwhile, beat the eggs well with the lemon juice, until frothy. Take the soup pan off the heat and let cool slightly before adding 4–5 tablespoons hot stock to egg mixture. Stir in well.

3. Pour the stock and rice into the top of a double boiler. Strain the egg mixture into the stock, and stir in well. Stir over gentle heat while the soup thickens. Do not boil, or the eggs will curdle.

4. When soup is creamy, add the lemon rind and adjust seasoning. If serving hot, pour into soup cups, put a spoonful of cream into each and sprinkle with chopped parsley. If serving cold, allow soup to cool, add the slightly whipped cream, then chill before serving.

Yogurt, Shrimp and Cucumber Soup

½ large cucumber, peeled and diced
1 cup natural yogurt
1½ cups chicken stock
1 cup tomato juice
1 clove garlic, crushed
1–2 teaspoons lemon juice
2 teaspoons chopped dill fennel, or
½ cup cooked shrimp
1 large tomato, peeled, and diced
2 tablespoons diced green pepper
1 cup cream

GARNISH
2 teaspoons chopped dill or fennel, or paprika
French bread and butter, or garlic bread (see garnish section)

Unusual summer cold soup made with yogurt, tomato juice, chicken stock and shrimp (Serves 4–6, cold)

1. Peel and dice the cucumber. Sprinkle with salt and leave covered for at least 20–30 minutes. Then drain and rinse with cold water. Put the yogurt, stock, tomato juice and crushed garlic into an electric blender and blend slowly until smooth, adding pepper, lemon juice and chopped dill or fennel when soup is well mixed.

2. Add the drained diced cucumber and shrimp, the diced tomato and diced pepper. Stir in cream, adjust seasoning and chill thoroughly.

3. Sprinkle with chopped dill or fennel or paprika, and serve with French bread or garlic bread.

Peanut Soup

2 tablespoons butter
1 small onion, finely chopped
½ cup of freshly roasted peanuts (or ¼ cup of peanut butter)
1 tablespoon flour
4–5 cups stock
¼ teaspoon Worcestershire sauce
a dash of chili sauce
a good squeeze of lemon juice

GARNISH
paprika
fried bread croutons (see garnish section)

Creamy golden-colored nut-flavored soup (Serves 4–6, hot)

1. Melt the butter and cook the onion gently for 2–3 minutes to soften. If using peanut butter, add this and then the flour. If using whole peanuts blend in an electric blender with one cup of stock and add to onions after the flour. Stir in the stock and mix well until smooth. Bring to boil. Then reduce heat, and simmer for about 20 minutes, stirring constantly to prevent soup from sticking to bottom of pan.

2. Add Worcestershire sauce, chili sauce, lemon juice, salt and pepper.

3. Serve hot with a garnish of paprika and fried bread croutons.

Iced Tomato and Cucumber Soup

A refreshing summer soup made with tomato juice, cucumber and seasonings (Serves 4–6, cold)

1 cucumber, peeled and diced
2 cans (about 16 oz each or 4 cups) tomato juice
1–2 teaspoons onion juice
1–1½ teaspoon Worcestershire sauce
½ teaspoon sugar
2–3 teaspoons lemon juice
a dash of tabasco

GARNISH
4–6 tablespoons sour cream
4–6 slices lemon
1 tablespoon chopped chives
brown bread and butter

1. Peel and dice the cucumber. Sprinkle with salt and leave covered for at least 20–30 minutes. Drain and rinse with cold water.

2. Put tomato juice into bowl and add the onion juice (made by crushing small pieces of onion in a garlic press). Add Worcestershire sauce, sugar, lemon juice, salt and pepper and a dash of tabasco.

3. Add the diced cucumber to tomato soup and ladle into soup cups. Chill thoroughly.

4. Garnish with a spoonful of sour cream and a thin slice of lemon or a sprinkling of chopped chives in each cup. Serve brown bread and butter separately.

Gazpacho

A traditional iced Spanish uncooked soup (Serves 4–6, cold)

4–6 large ripe red tomatoes
4–6 spring onions or 1 medium onion
1–2 cloves garlic
1 medium cucumber
1 green pepper
1 thick slice brown bread
1½ cups iced water
4 tablespoons good quality olive oil
2 tablespoons wine vinegar
1 tablespoon lemon juice
2 tablespoons chopped mixed parsley, basil, marjoram
a few ice cubes

GARNISH
fried garlic croutons (see garnish section)

1. Remove skins from tomatoes by dipping in boiling water for a count of 10, then in cold water, thus loosening skins. Chop tomatoes coarsely, removing hard cores. Reserve ¼ cup for garnish. Slice the white parts of spring onions or chop medium onion. Crush garlic, and mix with onions and tomatoes. Peel and dice cucumber, sprinkle with salt and let stand for 20–30 minutes, then wash well and drain. Add half to tomato mixture and reserve remainder for garnish. Remove stalk, pips and veins from green pepper and slice finely. Add three-quarters to soup and reserve rest for garnish. Soak the bread in half the iced water until really soft.

2. Put the tomato mixture into electric blender. Add olive oil, vinegar, lemon juice, the softened bread and some salt and pepper. Blend until smooth and strain if necessary through a coarse sieve.

3. Add the reserved vegetables to the soup, and chill thoroughly. Just before serving, add enough of the remaining iced water to thin to a desired consistency. Adjust seasoning, sprinkle with herbs and serve with a few small ice cubes in each soup cup and with fried garlic croutons.

Cherry Soup

A bitter-sweet rich red soup, good for summer (Serves 4–6, hot)

- 1½ lbs sweet red cherries (or canned equivalent)
- 4 cups water
- ½ cinnamon stick (or ¼ teaspoon ground cinnamon)
- 3–4 slivers of orange or lemon rind and juice of half an orange or lemon
- 1 cup red wine
- 1 tablespoon cornstarch
- sugar to taste

1. Pit the cherries and put about three-quarters of them into a pan. Cover with the water and add the cinnamon and lemon or orange rind, which must be very finely pared, and the juice of half an orange or lemon. Cover the pan and simmer gently until the cherries are tender.

2. Put the soup through a fine food mill or into an electric blender and blend until smooth. Add red wine.

3. Add the cornstarch to cold water and mix until smooth. Add a little hot soup to the cornstarch mixture and pour this back into the soup, stir in well then bring to a boil and cook for 4–5 minutes. Add the reserved cherries for the last few minutes to heat through.

4. Add sugar to taste and serve hot with crackers, which can be crumbled into the soup if desired.

Cranberry and Orange Soup

A delicious cold fruity soup for summer (Serves 4–6, cold–see picture, p. 59)

- 1 pound of fresh cranberries (or canned equivalent)
- 2 cups of light chicken stock (or water)
- 1½ cups white wine
- 2–3 pieces of lemon rind
- pared rind of a ripe orange
- ½ cinnamon stick
- ¼–½ cup sugar to taste
- juice of two oranges
- juice of ½ lemon
- 2 envelopes gelatine (if soup is to be jellied)

GARNISH

- 4–6 slices or orange

1. Wash the cranberries if fresh. Put into a pan with chicken stock (or water) and white wine. Add the pieces of lemon and orange rind and the cinnamon stick. Simmer for about 10 minutes, until the cranberries have softened.

2. Put the fruit and juice through a fine nylon sieve or the fine food mill after removing the cinnamon stick. Sweeten to taste and add the orange and lemon juice. (If using canned cranberries it may not be necessary to add any sugar as these are usually sweetened.)

3. This soup can also be served jellied if two envelopes of gelatine are softened in a little stock or water and then added after the soup has been sieved. It will then be necessary to re-heat the soup for a few minutes while blending in the gelatine.

4. Serve chilled or jellied with a thin slice of orange as a garnish.

Cold Buttermilk Soup

A very refreshing cold soup (Serves 4–6, cold)

- 2 large eggs
- grated rind and juice of 1 lemon (or vanilla extract)
- ¼ cup sugar
- 4 cups buttermilk
- ½ cup heavy cream

GARNISH

- grated rind of half a lemon or
- 2 tablespoons chopped and lightly browned almonds

1. Beat the egg yolks, lemon rind and juice (or vanilla) with the sugar until light and frothy. Beat the buttermilk, and stir into the egg yolk mixture.

2. Beat the egg whites stiff, adding a pinch of salt. Then whip the cream. Carefully fold the egg whites into the cream. Add this to the egg yolk and buttermilk. Do not blend too thoroughly but leave it rather lumpy in texture.

3. Ladle into soup cups. Then chill thoroughly, garnish with finely grated lemon rind or chopped almonds, and serve plain crackers separately.

9 MAIN DISH SOUPS

Black Bean Soup

1–1½ cups dried black beans
1 ham bone or some ham meat minus fat
5–6 cups water
2 medium onions, sliced
4–5 stalks celery, sliced
2–3 carrots, sliced
1 bay leaf, 5–6 sprigs parsley, 1 sprig thyme, tied together
2 cloves
½ teaspoon mustard powder
a pinch of cayenne pepper
stock or milk

GARNISH
2 hard-boiled eggs
4–6 slices lemon or ½ cup chopped ham
fried bread croutons (see garnish section)

A thick, filling winter soup, served by itself or with slices of bread and cheese (Serves 4–6, hot)

1. Wash beans in several changes of cold water then cover with cold water and soak overnight. Drain and put beans into a large thick pan. Add water, ham bone or pieces of ham, cover the pan and cook for 2 hours. Add the onions, celery and carrots, the herbs, cloves, mustard and cayenne pepper. Re-cover pan and cook for another 1–1½ hours or until beans are tender.

2. Remove the bone and herbs. Put the soup through a fine sieve or blend in electric blender. Re-heat soup and if too thick add enough stock or milk to make a good texture. Adjust seasoning.

3. Serve hot. Garnish with slices of hard-boiled egg and lemon slices or ½ cup chopped ham and fried bread croutons.

Ham Flavored Pea Soup

1 cup split peas
5–6 cups water
1 ham bone
1 onion, chopped
2 stalks celery, chopped
1 bay leaf
4–5 sprigs of parsley (or 1 large tablespoon dried parsley)
½ teaspoon sugar
¼ teaspoon ground pepper
2 tablespoons butter
1 tablespoon flour
a little mint

GARNISH
4–6 tablespoons cream
½–1 cup chopped ham (or 2–3 slices of bacon chopped and fried crisply)
fried bread croutons (see garnish section)

Thick pea soup made with dried peas and ham stock, garnished with chopped ham, a meal in itself (Serves 4–6, hot)

1. Start making this soup the day before it is required, as the split peas need to be soaked for 6–8 hours in cold water after being washed in several changes of cold water.

2. Next day wash the ham bone, and remove and discard any surplus fat. Put into a large pan with the split peas and the water in which they have been soaking. Add the onion, celery, bay leaf, parsley sprigs, sugar, black pepper and a little salt, remembering that the ham bone is likely to be salty. Cover and bring the soup to a boil; then simmer gently, until the peas are tender. Stir from time to time to prevent peas from sticking. This may take 1–2 hours.

3. Remove bay leaf and bones. Then put soup into electric blender and blend until smooth, or put through food mill.

4. Melt butter in rinsed out pan, stir in flour, and when blended pour on soup. Stir until smoothly blended, then bring to a boil, stirring constantly. Simmer for a few minutes. Adjust seasoning, and add mint and a little more water if soup is too thick.

5. Serve hot with a spoon of cream on top of each serving and a garnish of chopped ham or fried bacon bits, or fried bread croutons.

Tripe Soup

½ pound cooked honeycomb tripe
3–4 cups chicken or white stock
2 potatoes, chopped
2 onions, chopped
2–3 stalks celery, chopped
3 tablespoons butter
1½ tablespoons flour
1 tablespoon chopped parsley
1 teaspoon marjoram
a pinch of thyme
a pinch of cayenne pepper

GARNISH
2 tablespoons butter
½ cup cream
fried bread croutons (see garnish section)

Traditional soup, somewhat simplified for modern kitchens, based on old-style Philadelphia pepper pot soup (Serves 6, hot)

1. Buy ready cooked tripe or canned tripe, and cut into small cubes. Cook gently in the chicken or white stock for about 1 hour, with pepper and salt if necessary.

2. Meanwhile, cook the potatoes, onions and celery in melted butter in tightly-covered soup pot until tender, shaking to prevent sticking and burning, about 12–15 minutes. Then blend in the flour until smooth.

3. When the tripe is cooked, strain the liquid into the vegetables and stir to mix in well. Bring slowly to a boil, stirring until smooth. Add the tripe and the chopped herbs and cayenne pepper. Simmer together for a few minutes. Adjust seasoning. Add some butter and cream just before serving.

4. Serve hot with fried bread croutons.

Cock-a-Leekie Soup

1 small stewing chicken
1 onion
2 carrots
1 stalk celery
6 peppercorns
1 bay leaf
1 sprig of thyme (or ¼ teaspoon dried thyme)
6–8 sprigs of parsley
1 sprig of tarragon (or ¼ teaspoon dried tarragon)
4–6 leeks, white part only
2 carrots, sliced
2 tablespoons rice
1 tablespoon chopped parsley

A rich chicken broth with rice and vegetables, a meal in itself (Serves 6–8, hot)

1. Put the chicken in water with 1 onion, 2 carrots and 1 stalk of celery. Add peppercorns, herbs and salt. Simmer for 1½–2 hours or until the chicken is really tender. Remove chicken and strain stock, which will be reserved for soup.

2. While chicken cooks, wash and slice white part of leeks and soak in salted water to remove grit. Then drain well. Put leeks and carrots in a soup pot and add 6 cups of stock from cooked chicken. Cook for 10 minutes. Then add rice and continue cooking for 10–15 minutes.

3. Add some meat from the cooked chicken to the soup with the chopped parsley. Re-heat and serve hot with wholewheat bread and butter. Remaining chicken can be used for another dish.

Chicken Gumbo

1 large or 2 smaller onions, chopped
3 tablespoons butter or bacon fat
1½ cups canned tomatoes
½ green pepper, seeded and chopped
¾–1 cup canned okra (or ready-cooked okra)
2 tablespoons rice
4–5 cups strongly-flavored chicken stock made with whole chicken
1–2 cups chopped cooked chicken
1 tablespoon chopped parsley
1 teaspoon chopped tarragon
½ cup cooked corn (optional)

GARNISH
fried bread croutons (see garnish section)

A well-flavored chicken soup rich with vegetables and rice (Serves 4–6, hot)

1. Melt the butter or bacon fat in a soup pot and cook the onion gently for 5–6 minutes with the lid on until tender but not brown. Add the chopped tomatoes, chopped pepper, okra and rice. Pour in stock and mix thoroughly. Add salt and pepper if necessary. Cover the pan and simmer until the vegetables are tender, about 20–30 minutes.

2. Adjust seasoning and add the chopped cooked chicken and herbs. If available, ½ cup of cooked corn can also be added. Re-heat and serve hot.

3. This soup can be served on its own as a main course and then it is nice to serve fried bread croutons or thick bread and butter with it.

Mulligatawny Soup

1 large onion, chopped
1 carrot, chopped
1–2 stalks celery, chopped
1 medium sour cooking apple
3–4 tablespoons butter (or oil)
1 tablespoon curry powder (or paste)
1½ tablespoon flour
1 tablespoon tomato purée
4–5 cups stock
1 bay leaf
3–4 sprigs of parsley
a pinch of thyme
2 tablespoons shredded coconut
1 teaspoon sugar
2 teaspoons lemon juice
4–6 tablespoons cooked rice

GARNISH
4–6 slices of lemon
paprika

A fairly thick curry soup with cooked rice, garnished with lemon (Serves 4–6, hot)

1. Melt butter or oil and add the onion, carrot, celery and apple, stir well and cook gently for 5–6 minutes. Add the curry powder or paste, and cook for a few more minutes. Add the flour, mixing well, and cook for a few minutes to brown slightly. Add the tomato purée and the stock. Blend well before bringing slowly to a boil. Reduce the heat. Add herbs, seasoning, coconut and sugar. Simmer for 30–45 minutes with lid on pan.
2. Remove bay leaf, then blend soup in electric blender or put through fine food mill. Return to pan, add rice and adjust seasoning. Re-heat, adding lemon juice just before serving. (If preferred the rice can be served separately.)
3. Serve hot with a slice of lemon and sprinkled with paprika.

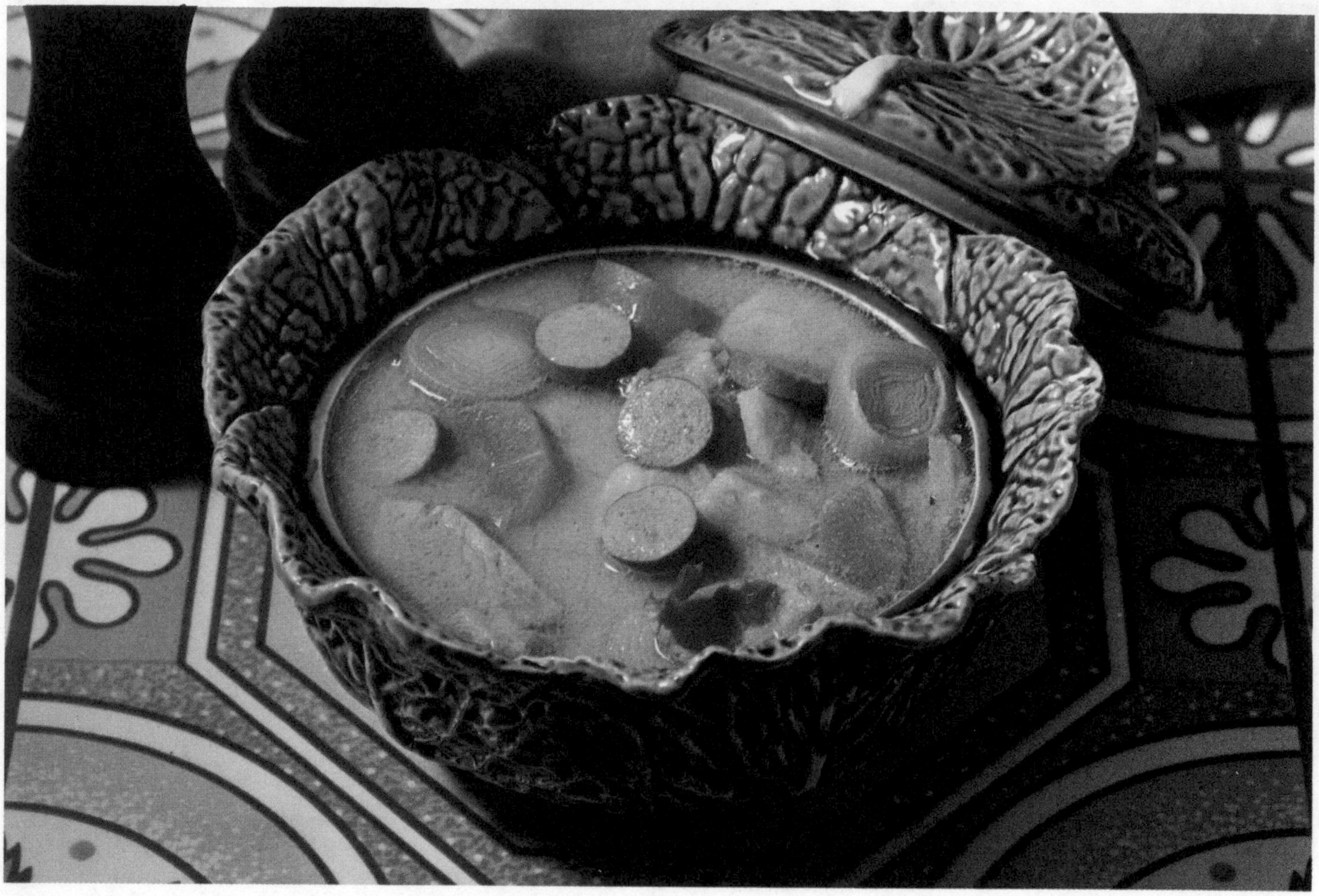

Cabbage Soup

1 small green cabbage (or 2 cups of shredded green cabbage)
1 large onion, chopped
2 small leeks, white part only, sliced
2 carrots, sliced
1 potato, sliced
2 slices fat bacon
1 tablespoon flour
4 cups brown stock (or water and cubes—ham stock can be used, if not too salt)
2 tablespoons chopped parsley
1 bay leaf
a pinch of nutmeg
2 teaspoons of chopped dill or 1 teaspoon dill seeds

GARNISH
3–4 frankfurters
fat for frying
fried bread and bacon croutons (see garnish section)

A very filling vegetable soup garnished with sliced cooked sausages. A meal in a soup (Serves 4–6, hot)

1. Slice and wash the green cabbage, put into a pan of boiling salted water, and cook for 5 minutes. Then drain and rinse under cold water.

2. Meanwhile, chop the bacon and heat over gentle heat until the fat runs. Then add the onion, leeks, carrots and potato, and stir over heat for a few minutes. Sprinkle in flour, and blend well before adding stock (or water and cubes). Add parsley, bay leaf, salt and pepper. Bring to a boil. Then reduce heat, and simmer for 10 minutes before adding cabbage. Cook for 20 minutes more, or until the vegetables are tender but not mushy.

3. Adjust seasoning, and add nutmeg and chopped dill, or a few dill seeds. Remove bay leaf.

4. For garnish, either fry frankfurters and cut in slices, putting a few slices into each serving, or prepare fried bread and bacon croutons to serve separately.

Yellow Pea Soup

1 cup split yellow peas
5 cups water
1 ham bone
2 onions, sliced
1 cup chopped celery or celeriac
2 carrots, sliced
1 small potato, sliced
1 bay leaf, several sprigs of parsley, 1 sprig thyme, tied together
½–1 cup chopped ham
2 tablespoons parsley

GARNISH
fried bread croutons (see garnish section)

Thick ham-flavored yellow pea soup, very filling, garnished with chopped ham (Serves 6–8, hot)

1. Wash and soak the split peas overnight if not using a quick cooking variety. Drain and put into a pan, with 5 cups water, the ham bone, vegetables, bay leaf, parsley sprigs and some salt and pepper. Bring to a boil. Then simmer for 1½–2 hours or until peas and vegetables are tender.

2. Remove the ham bone and herbs, and put the soup into electric blender and blend until smooth. Measure soup and bring it up to the required quantity with water or stock. Taste and adjust seasoning. Re-heat, adding the chopped ham.

3. Sprinkle with chopped parsley, and serve with fried croutons.

Scotch Broth

A very filling meaty soup full of vegetables and pearl barley (Serves 6–8, hot)

3–4 tablespoons pearl barley
1½–2 pounds neck or breast of mutton or lamb
6–8 cups water
1 teaspoon salt
¼ teaspoon pepper
1 bay leaf
2 large onions, one to add whole, the other diced for garnish
1 clove
3 carrots, one sliced for the soup, 2 diced for garnish
4 stalks celery, 2 whole for the soup, 2 diced for garnish
½ small turnip, diced for garnish
1 leek, sliced for garnish
2 tablespoons chopped parsley

1. Soak barley for several hours, preferably overnight, in cold water.

2. Remove as much fat as possible from the lamb or mutton and put into a soup pot with the water and the drained barley. Add salt and pepper, the bay leaf, herbs, a whole onion stuck with a clove, a sliced carrot and 2 stalks of celery. Bring slowly to a boil and simmer for 1½ hours, skimming off the fat and scum occasionally.

3. If time allows let soup cool and skim off fat; if not, skim carefully while hot, removing the bay leaf and celery and carrot as far as possible.

4. Add the diced vegetables and cook for 20–30 minutes or until they are tender. Adjust seasoning of soup and if too much liquid has evaporated add a little extra to make up quantity. Remove the bones, leaving the meat in the soup. Re-heat and serve hot sprinkled with chopped parsley.

Lentil Soup

Thick winter ham-flavored soup, served with hot sausages or chopped ham and fried croutons (Serves 4–6, hot)

1 cup red lentils
1 large or 2 smaller onions, chopped
2 small carrots, chopped
2 stalks celery, chopped
2 tablespoons butter or bacon fat
1 ham bone
1 bay leaf, 4–5 sprigs of parsley, 1 sprig thyme, tied together
a little sugar
1 teaspoon tomato pureé

GARNISH
fried bread croutons (see garnish section)
chopped cooked sausages
½ cup chopped ham
2 tablespoons chopped parsley

1. Wash the lentils several times. Then cover with cold water and soak for 4–6 hours or overnight. If used unsoaked the cooking time has to be considerably increased as does the amount of water used, as it evaporates during cooking.

2. Cook the onion, carrots and celery in the melted butter for 5–6 minutes to soften. Then add the drained lentils and the ham bone. Add the bay leaf, parsley sprigs, thyme, pepper and a little sugar. Bring to a boil. Then cover and simmer until tender. This will take at least 2 hours or longer, depending on the type of lentils.

3. Remove the herbs, and put soup through a fine food mill or into the electric blender and blend until smooth, adding tomato purée. If the soup is too thick at this stage, bring it up to the required quantity with stock or water. Adjust seasoning, adding salt if necessary.

4. Serve hot with fried bread croutons, chopped cooked sausages or chopped ham. Sprinkle with chopped parsley.

Borsch or Russian Beet Soup

A rich red beet soup thick with vegetables and very filling, a meal in itself (Serves 4–6, hot)

3 medium beets
1 onion, sliced
2 carrots, shredded
½ small turnip, shredded
½ small parsnip, shredded
2 stalks celery, sliced
6 cups well-flavored brown or household stock
1 bay leaf
3–4 sprigs of parsley
½ small cabbage, shredded
1–2 tablespoons tomato purée
2 teaspoons lemon juice
1–2 tablespoons mixed chopped parsley, dill and basil

GARNISH
6 tablespoons sour cream
3–4 cooked frankfurters or other sausages

1. Peel and cut two of the beets into thin, short strips. Place in soup pot with onion, carrots, turnip, parsnip and celery. Cover with stock, and add herbs and seasoning. Cook gently without boiling for 30–35 minutes.

2. Meanwhile, wash the cabbage and drain thoroughly. Add cabbage and tomato purée to the soup. Simmer until cabbage is tender but not overcooked.

3. While the soup cooks, grate the remaining beet into a small pan, cover with a cup of hot stock and add the lemon juice to make the beet juice run. Heat gently for a few minutes but do not boil as this will ruin the good red color. Strain this juice into the soup, adjust seasoning and add the chopped herbs.

4. Serve hot with a spoonful of sour cream and hot slices frankfurter or other cooked sausage in each soup plate. (This soup improves by being made a day before being served and re-heated carefully.)

Cheese Soup

Delicious cheesy thick soup (Serves 5–6, hot)

3 tablespoons butter
2 slices of bacon, chopped
1 large or 2 small onions, chopped
2–3 stalks celery, chopped
1 cup fresh white breadcrumbs
4–5 cups stock or consomme
a pinch of cayenne pepper
1 bay leaf, 3–4 sprigs of parsley, tied together
½–¾ cup Parmesan or other strongly flavored hard cheese
a pinch of dry mustard

OPTIONAL GARNISH
2 egg yolks
½ cup cream
fried bread croutons (see garnish section)
paprika

1. Cook bacon, onion and celery gently in melted butter stirring frequently until the onions are golden brown. Add the fresh bread crumbs and mix well before adding the stock or consomme. Add seasoning, cayenne pepper, bay leaf and parsley sprigs. Bring the whole mixture to a boil, stirring constantly. Cover and simmer for about 20 minutes. Remove the bay leaf and parsley.

2. Add the cheese and mix well. A little dry mustard can also be added. This soup can be made richer by adding a mixture of egg yolks and cream if preferred.

3. Sprinkle with paprika and serve hot with croutons.

Kidney Soup

3 lamb kidneys or ½ pound ox kidney
salted water to cover kidneys for soaking
2–3 tablespoons butter or oil
2 onions, chopped
2 carrots, sliced
2 stalks celery, sliced
1½ tablespoons flour
1 tablespoon tomato purée
5 cups beef or brown stock
1 teaspoon Worcestershire sauce
several sprigs of parsley, 1 sprig thyme, 1 bay leaf, tied together
1 cup sliced mushrooms
a dash of tabasco or chili sauce
a little gravy mix, beef bouillon or soy sauce
2–3 tablespoons sherry
2 tablespoons chopped parsley

GARNISH
fried bread croutons (see garnish section)

Rich, filling, meaty soup, served with fried croutons to make a hearty winter meal (Serves 4–6, hot)

1. Remove the skin and cores from kidneys and cut into small pieces. Put to soak for a few minutes in cold, slightly salted water to remove any strong flavor. Drain.

2. Melt the butter and cook the onions, carrots and celery for a few minutes, stirring well. Add the kidney and cook for 6–7 minutes to brown all the ingredients lightly. Sprinkle in flour and mix well. Add the tomato purée, stock and Worcestershire sauce. Bring to a boil slowly, stirring constantly. Add herbs and seasoning. Then cover pan and simmer for about 45 minutes or until the kidney and vegetables are tender. Remove herbs.

3. Just before the end of the cooking time add the sliced mushrooms and a dash of tabasco or chili sauce. Adjust seasoning, and if soup is not a good color, add a little gravy mix, beef bouillon or soy sauce.

4. Just before serving, add the sherry and sprinkle with chopped parsley. Serve with fried croutons.

Fresh Corn Chowder

2 potatoes, peeled and diced
1½ cups fresh corn
3 cups salted water
½ green pepper, seeded and chopped
3 tablespoons butter or bacon fat
1 onion, chopped
2 stalks celery, chopped
2 tablespoons flour
2 cups milk
1 bay leaf, 3–4 sprigs of parsley, tied together
¼ teaspoon mace or nutmeg
½ cup cream

GARNISH
2 tablespoons chopped parsley
fried bread croutons or cheesy croutons (see garnish section)

A filling creamy chowder with corn, potato, pepper and celery all blended together (Serves 4–6, hot)

1. Pre-cook the diced potatoes together with the fresh corn in 3 cups of lightly salted water until tender, or about 6–8 minutes. Then strain carefully, reserving 2 cups of the water for chowder.

2. Melt the butter or bacon fat and cook the pepper, onion and celery for 6–7 minutes, until golden brown. Sprinkle in the flour and blend thoroughly, then add the 2 cups of reserved potato water. Mix this in thoroughly and add the milk, bay leaf, parsley sprigs, salt, pepper and mace or nutmeg. Bring to a boil and add the pepper. Cook for 2–3 minutes.

3. Add the potato and corn, remove from heat, and allow the flavors to blend for at least 10–15 minutes. Then remove herbs. Re-heat chowder, and adjust seasoning. At the last minute add the cream, and re-heat without boiling.

4. Sprinkle with chopped parsley or paprika, and serve with fried bread croutons or cheesy croutons.

10 QUICK CANNED SOUPS

Quick Tomato Consomme

2 cups jellied chicken consomme
2 cups tomato juice
1 teaspoon tomato purée
¼ teaspoon sugar
2 teaspoons lemon juice
1 tablespoon gelatine
½ cup extra consomme (or water)
4 tablespoons white wine
red vegetable coloring (if needed)

GARNISH
4–6 lemon slices
1 bunch watercress
cheese straws or garlic bread (see garnish section)

Canned consomme and tomato juice combined to make a jellied soup (Serves 4–6, cold)

1. Put the canned consomme, tomato juice, tomato purée and sugar into a pot with lemon juice and bring slowly to a boil.

2. Put gelatine into a small pan with a little water and when it has swelled dissolve over gentle heat. Remove hot soup from heat and add gelatine.

3. Strain soup through muslin and a fine sieve. Adjust seasoning. When almost cold, add the white wine and the additional consomme or water. If the color is not good, add a little vegetable coloring.

4. Pour into soup cups and let chill. Decorate the top of each cup with a lemon slice or a little watercress. Serve with cheese straws or garlic bread.

Two-Tone Tomato and Chicken Soup

2 cans chicken (or beef) consomme
½ can of tomato juice
1 tablespoon tomato purée
a little lemon juice
a little sugar
1½ tablespoons gelatine
2–3 tablespoons sherry

GARNISH
4–6 slices of lemon or several watercress sprigs

Canned jellied chicken consomme and tomato consomme, chilled and mixed (Serves 4–6, cold)

1. Mix 1 can of chicken consomme with ½ can of tomato juice and the tomato purée. Add 1 tablespoon gelatine to a little of this mixture and allow to swell. Dissolve over very low heat and then add to the rest of the tomato consomme along with the lemon juice, sugar and seasoning. Mix thoroughly and let chill.

2. Add ½ tablespoon gelatine to the other can of consomme, allow to swell and then heat gently to dissolve. Add the sherry and let set separately from the first consomme.

3. Just before serving, spoon some of each consomme into each soup cup, alternating them so that it looks attractive. Serve with lemon slices or watercress sprigs.

Tomato and Horseradish Soup

1 can of condensed tomato soup
1 can stock (or water)
1–1½ teaspoons fresh horseradish (or ¼–½ teaspoon dried horseradish)
2 teaspoons tomato purée
1 tablespoon chopped parsley
2 teaspoons basil
1 teaspoon sugar

GARNISH
4 tablespoons heavy cream
1 tablespoon chopped parsley
cheese croutons (or cheese straws) (see garnish section)

A way of making canned tomato soup taste home-made (Serves 4, hot)

1. Pour the soup into a pan and add a can of stock or water. Add the horseradish, tomato purée, parsley, basil, sugar, salt and pepper. Bring to a boil and serve with a spoon of cream in each cup and a sprinkling of chopped parsley on top.

2. Serve with cheese croutons or cheese straws.

Boula

2–3 cups of green turtle soup
2–3 cups of green pea soup (if using condensed soup, use equal quantities of soup and water)
4 tablespoon sherry
4–6 tablespoons heavy cream
cayenne pepper

GARNISH
cheese straws (see garnish section)

A party soup made by combining canned green turtle and pea soup (Serves 4–6, hot)

1. Heat the canned soups together gently, blending thoroughly. Add seasoning and sherry just before serving.
2. Serve in soup cups with a large spoonful of whipped cream on each one, and sprinkle a little cayenne pepper on top of the cream. Serve at once with cheese straws.

Iced Tomato Soup Louise

1 can of condensed tomato soup
1–2 cans milk
1 cup ricotta (or cottage) cheese
a little grated onion
1–2 teaspoons grated horseradish
lemon juice to taste
a little sugar

GARNISH
4–6 tablespoons whipped cream
chopped chives or paprika
cheese straws (see garnish section)

Delicious, original, tangy cold tomato and cheese soup (Serves 4–6, cold)

1. Blend the canned soup with the milk and cheese. Add the grated onion, horseradish, lemon juice, sugar and seasoning. Blend again until smooth.
2. Chill well. Serve in soup cups with a spoonful of whipped cream in center of each cup and sprinkled with chopped chives or paprika.
3. Serve with cheese straws.

Canned Corn Chowder

1 small can of corn and pimento mixed
1 can of condensed chicken or celery soup
1 teaspoon of onion powder or de-hydrated onion
a pinch of sugar
1 teaspoon of curry powder (optional)
1½–2 cups milk
½ chicken cube
¼–½ cup cream
1 tablespoon butter

GARNISH
1 tablespoon chopped parsley

A quickly made, filling corn chowder, which can be flavored with curry if desired (Serves 4, hot)

1. Mix the can of soup with the can of mixed corn and pimento. Add the onion powder or dehydrated onion, salt, pepper, a pinch of sugar and, if desired, 1 teaspoon curry powder.
2. Heat together, adding the milk and the chicken cube. Cook gently for 5–6 minutes without boiling. Just before serving, add a little cream and put a small lump of butter on top of each soup cup. Sprinkle with chopped parsley, and serve with plain crackers.

Cranberry and Orange Soup (see p. 48)

Cold Asparagus Soup

A delicious quick soup made from cans (Serves 4, cold)

1 can of condensed asparagus soup
milk
1 can green asparagus tips
1 carton natural yogurt
a little lemon juice
a few drops of tabasco
¼ cup heavy cream
paprika

GARNISH
cheese straws (see garnish section)

1. Blend the condensed asparagus soup with the liquid from the can of asparagus tips using enough milk to fill the soup can.
2. Stir in the yogurt, or blend in an electric blender. Add a little lemon juice and a few drops of tabasco.
3. Stir in the asparagus tips and serve chilled with a spoonful of whipped cream in each cup. Sprinkle with paprika and serve with cheese straws.

Baked Bean and Tomato Soup

Tomato and baked bean soup garnished with crisp fried bacon (Serves 4–6, hot)

1 cup baked beans in tomato sauce
1 can condensed tomato soup
1 can tomato juice
1 can water
1 tablespoon tomato purée
½ teaspoon sugar
1 tablespoon chopped parsley

GARNISH
2–3 slices bacon

1. Put half a can of baked beans in pan with tomato soup, tomato juice, water, tomato purée and seasonings. Heat together gently, adding the chopped parsley. When well mixed and hot put into electric blender and blend until smooth.
2. Return to pan and heat, adding the remaining beans. Serve hot with the bacon, which has been fried until crisp, sprinkled on top.

Orange and Canned Tomato Soup

Tomato soup flavored with orange, which gives a delicious fresh flavor (Serves 4, hot)

1 orange
½ lemon
1 can of condensed tomato soup
1 can stock or water
a little sugar

1. Remove the rind from the orange and lemon with a potato peeler. Cut into match-like strips. Put these into boiling water for 1 minute, then drain and rinse with cold water.

2. Put can of soup in a pan with stock or water, add sugar, salt and pepper and heat, stirring until smooth. For the last few minutes add the orange and lemon rind and lastly the juice of the orange and ½ lemon.

Mock Crab Bisque

A delicious, quickly made party soup for unexpected guests (Serves 4–6, hot)

1 can tomato soup
1 can green pea soup
1 can milk or light cream
1 small can of crab meat or shrimp
2–3 tablespoons sherry
1 tablespoon butter

GARNISH
4–6 tablespoons heavy cream
1 tablespoon chopped parsley
or sprinkling of paprika

1. Mix the cans of soup in an electric blender, slowly adding the milk or cream.

2. Put into a soup pot and heat without boiling. When really hot, add the canned crab meat or shrimp and re-heat, adding the sherry and butter at the last minute.

3. Serve hot with a spoonful of heavy cream in each cup and sprinkled with chopped parsley or paprika.

Canned Pea Soup with Bacon

A delicious way of making canned pea soup taste home-made (Serves 4–6, hot)

1 can of condensed pea soup or two cans of ordinary pea soup
1 can of water or milk
2 slices of bacon
4 tablespoon cooked peas
4 tablespoon heavy cream
1 tablespoon chopped mint

GARNISH
fried bread croutons (see garnish section)

1. Chop the bacon slices, and cook gently until crisp. Add the pea soup and a can of water or milk. Stir over gentle heat until smooth. Then add the cooked peas. Heat to boiling point.

2. Pour into heated soup cups and put a spoonful of heavy cream into the center of each one. Sprinkle with chopped mint and serve at once with fried bread croutons. page 121

11 GARNISHES

Bacon Croutons

(For 4)

2 slices bacon
2 large slices white bread cut into cubes
oil
pepper

1. Remove rinds from bacon slices and chop the bacon finely. Put into a dry frying pan and cook slowly to extract fat, then cook until crisp and golden. Remove bacon bits and reserve.

2. Add enough oil to bacon fat to cook the diced bread in same way as fried bread croutons (see p. 63). When golden brown, remove and drain. Add the bacon bits with pepper and serve hot.

Cheese Croutons

(For 4)

2–3 slices white bread
2 tablespoons butter (approximately)
a little mustard or vegetable extract
4–6 tablespoons grated Italian cheese
cayenne pepper

1. Toast bread slices on one side only. Let cool. Then butter the reverse side and spread with a little mustard. Sprinkle thickly with the grated cheese, and with a little salt and pepper.

2. Broil until cheese is melted and browned. Sprinkle with cayenne pepper. When slightly cooled cut into squares or fingers. Serve hot.

Fried Bread Croutons

(For 4)

2 large slices white bread
oil
1 tablespoon butter
onion powder (as desired)

1. Remove crusts from slices of bread and cut the bread into small cubes. Heat enough oil in frying pan to come at least half way up the sides of the bread cubes while cooking. When the oil is hot, add the butter. When this has melted and is foaming, add all the bread cubes at once.

2. Cook over a moderate-to-hot flame and stir constantly to ensure that the cubes brown evenly. When golden brown, place on kitchen paper to drain. Remove from pan when slightly less brown than the final color you want as they continue to cook for a few seconds, because of the hot oil.

3. Season with salt and pepper, and onion powder, if this will improve the soup for which the croutons are intended. Keep hot and serve separately.

Garlic Croutons

(For 4)

1 clove garlic or ¾ teaspoon dried or powdered garlic
3 slices white bread
oil
cayenne pepper

1. Crush the garlic. Cut the crusts off bread slices and cut into cubes. Heat the oil. When hot add the bread cubes and cook, stirring constantly. When cubes start to turn color add the garlic and mix well. When cubes are golden brown remove and drain.

2. Sprinkle with salt and pepper and a touch of cayenne pepper, and serve hot.

Garlic Bread

1 long French loaf
3–4 tablespoon butter
1–2 cloves garlic
salt and pepper to taste
1 teaspoon oregano (optional)

1. Cut a long French loaf into slanting slices without quite cutting through the bottom of loaf. Soften the butter and mix in the crushed garlic and seasonings. Spread this mixture between the slices. Close the loaf and wrap in foil.

2. Put into medium oven to heat through for about 10 minutes, then open the foil and allow the bread to crisp for about 2 minutes.

Cheese Straws

Light cheesy crackers or straws which go well with a variety of soups (For 4)

½ cup of butter or 1 stick
1 cup of all purpose flour
1 cup grated American cheese
¼ teaspoon dry mustard
cayenne pepper and salt to taste

1. Cut the butter into the flour which has been sifted into a bowl. Blend well. Add the grated cheese, dry mustard, pepper, cayenne pepper, and salt if necessary. Shape the paste into a ball, wrap well and refrigerate for at least 10 minutes.

2. Roll out paste on a floured board and cut into strips or rounds. Bake in a hot oven (400°) for 6–10 minutes or until golden brown and crisp.

Sausage or Hamburger Balls

A filling addition which makes soup into a meal (Serves 6, hot)

1 thick slice of white bread without crusts
½ cup cold water
½ pound of sausage meat or ground raw beef
1 small chopped onion
1 clove garlic
1—2 tablespoons butter
1 tablespoon chopped parsley
¼ teaspoon thyme and oregano
1 teaspoon Worcestershire sauce
2 teaspoons tomato sauce
a dash of tabasco
1 beaten egg

1. Soak the bread in cold water. Put the sausage meat or ground beef into a bowl. Squeeze the water from the bread and add to the meat. Mix with a fork.

2. Chop the onion and crush the garlic. Melt the butter and cook onion and garlic gently until golden brown, about 6—7 minutes. Add this to the meat together with parsley, thyme, oregano and the sauces. Add seasoning to taste and enough of the beaten egg to hold the mixture together. Mix thoroughly.

3. Take the mixture by large teaspoonful and roll into balls. Cook these in boiling stock or soup for about 15 minutes, or roll in seasoned flour and fry gently in butter or oil for about the same length of time.

4. Add to any meat or vegetable soup as a filling garnish.

Piroshki for Beet Soups

(For 4)

2 tablespoons butter
1 small onion finely chopped
4—6 mushrooms
2—3 tablespoons cooked rice
2 tablespoons cooked chopped ham
1 tablespoon chopped parsley
1 small package of frozen flaky pastry (thawed)
1 beaten egg

1. Melt butter and cook finely chopped onion for 2—3 minutes to soften, then add mushrooms and cook for 4 more minutes. Add cooked rice and ham. Season with salt and pepper, and add chopped parsley. Cool before using.

2. Roll out the puff pastry into a long strip about 1½ inches in width or wider if larger piroshki are desired. Using a 1½ inch cutter, cut out as many rounds as possible.

3. Put a teaspoon of the cooled filling into the center of each pastry circle. Moisten the edges and press together to form a crescent shaped pie or piroshki. Brush the top with beaten egg and bake in a hot oven for 10—15 minutes until golden brown and crisp. Serve hot with beet soup.

4. Other ingredients can be used in piroshki such as smoked salmon, diced chicken, or small quantities of left-over meat.

List of additional Garnishes

1. Chopped parsley
2. Other chopped herbs
3. Chopped chives or young green onion tops
4. Watercress sprigs
5. Slices of lemon
6. Olives, sliced
7. Yogurt
8. Shreds of orange rind
9. Shreds of lemon rind
10. Slices of cucumber
11. Cooked shrimp
12. Browned almonds or peanuts
13. Rice plainly boiled or colored with turmeric or paprika
14. Popcorn
15. Crumbled bacon bits
16. Whipped cream
17. Sour cream
18. Crumbled potato chips
19. Grated cheese
20. Grated nutmeg
21. Paprika
22. Slices of avocado
23. Sliced cooked sausages or frankfurters
24. Chopped cooked ham
25. Canned devilled ham
26. Cooked noodles
27. Alphabet noodles
28. Hard-boiled eggs, sliced or sieved
29. Royale custard (see p. 39)